15 Minutes a Day

Raise the Bar to

As, Bs, & Honor Roll

Dr. Francisca Enih

Copyright © 2021 Francisca Enih
All Rights Reserved

Year of the Book
135 Glen Avenue
Glen Rock, PA 17327

Print ISBN: 978-1-64649-134-6
Ebook ISBN: 978-1-64649-135-3

This work may not be reproduced in any form, stored in any retrieval system, or transmitted in any form by any means—electronic, mechanical, photocopy, recording, or otherwise—without prior written permission of the author, except as provided by United States of America copyright law. For permission requests, write to the publisher.

Photos licensed for commercial use through depositphotos.com

Cover design by Pixelstudio

Advance Praise

"Practical, insightful, and compassionate, expressing a genuine concern for the education of our children and providing them and their parents with the tools to excel."

—PATRICK J. DYER

"A must-read book for all parents. Dr. Enih is a veteran teacher of various subjects in Houston public school at all levels. This book presents proven strategies and tips to help your child succeed in school. With our current educational system of virtual learning, this work is a timely contribution. Your child is more likely to succeed in school with parental support and guidance. Parent will learn how to handle concerns in the areas of homework, outside activities, teacher's relationship, goals, testing, study habits, health, learning tricks, motivation, discipline and many more. Success in school leads to a happy, successful and productive life—three things we as parents all want for our children."

—CATHERINE OBASUYI, M.Ed., LPC, LMFT, LCDC

"Dr. Francisca Enih has raised three beautiful, high-achieving children and now offers tools and tips from the wealth of her years as a master teacher."

—PAT O'CONNOR

"This book should be wrapped as a gift for every parent registering their children in 1st grade and 6th grade. It is a counter to the adage: 'Children do not come with instructions.' This is a parent/teacher/admin/guardian playbook for success."

—LATIFAT AGBOOLA SAAKA

Dedication

To my family: The love of my life, most amazing, selfless, God-praising, family loving man. I am blessed to live my life with you forever, the one and only darling husband, Sir Francis Enih, and our three beautiful, intelligent and caring children, Chijioke, Chinwendu and Chinyere Enih. Words cannot express how much I love you for the guidance you've shown me, for your wisdom, keen insight, taste, strength, integrity and humility. A special thank you to our grandchildren Sabria Enih and Cameron Nwagwu.

The two I have known and loved for longer, and more closely than any others, are my parents—Chief Gabriel Igboekwu and Mrs. Bernadette Igboekwu.

Acknowledgments

With gratitude to my family—Sir Francis Enih, Engr.; Chijioke Anthony Enih; Dr. Monique Enih; and Miss Christine Chinyere Enih.

Thanks to the many friends who discussed topics contained in this book. Your insight is greatly appreciated: Sir/Engr Festus & Lady Stella Igboekwu, Sylvanus I. O. Anidu, Dr. Chris Agho-Otoghile, Dr. Veronica Okon Achibong, Mrs. Amaebi Ikemi, Mrs. Mary Magdalene Ibekaku, Mrs. Augustina Ogbu, Engr. Georgina Boi, Mrs. Patricia Nwanze, Sir/Engr. Emmanuel & Nkechi Igboekwu, Hon. Benjamin & Florence Igboekwu, Aunty Ann Aniekwe, Ms. Latifat Agboola Saaka, Mrs. Catherine Obasuyi, Pat O'Connor, Patrick J. Dyer, Mrs. J. Akilo, Mrs. Caroline Ikwueze, Mrs. Beatrice Jideofor, Mr. Joseph S. Adejumo, Anthony Ogbo Ph.D., Ezeagu Women's Association of Houston, Mrs. Virginia Ndu, Dr. Femi & Pastor Helen Adetunji.

I wish to thank my colleagues and administrators at Holland MS, especially my first principal Ms. Adele Rogers, my mentor Mrs. Patricia Clark, Mr. Larry Martin, and Mr. Craig Edgley for your confidence in my work, and your patience and help.

I would also like to say a special thank you to Dr. Monique Enih, Dr. Demi Stevens, and Dr. Russell Strickland for their love, support, vision and assisting with this publication, and for keeping me on schedule.

Contents

Preface 1
1 | Academic Excellence 5
2 | Parental Involvement 15
3 | Conducive Atmosphere for Educational Success 21
4 | Parental Moral Support 27
5 | Monitoring and Assisting with School Assignments ... 35
6 | Advocating for Your Child at School 45
7 | Supervising the Academic Success of Your Child 53
8 | Encouraging Academic Performance 67
9 | Demographics and Parental Involvement 73
10 | Conclusion 85
References 99

GET YOUR 15 MINUTES A DAY
FREE BONUS CHECKLIST
Get on Track for As, Bs, & Honor Roll...

QUICK AND EASY

- Put Your Bedtime Routine on Autopilot, so that you rest easy at the end of the day

- Develop Responsibility in Your Child, so that he or she can drive his or her own progress

- Connect with Your Child Each Day, so that you can understand what's really important to them

- Organize Your Morning Routine, so that your child is ready to Win the Day

- Instill a Positive Work Ethic in Your Child, so that they are ready to suceed at home & at school

- Reward Yourself & Your Child, so that you are both motivated to make these new habits permanent

Total Value: $127 worth of bonuses!

15MinutesADayBook.com/Win

PREFACE

When parents say encouraging words long enough to their child, confidence starts to become a part of the child's belief system. The parents also generally wish they had instilled this confidence in their child from a younger age.

As a secondary school teacher, I have seen many well-performing students in all contexts from different backgrounds. They range from European-American, Asian-American, and African-American to Hispanic, male and female, and from different socio-economic backgrounds. Students transition from elementary to secondary school with an ever-increasing sense of independence and personal authority.

Secondary school is a special time in a student's life, filled with developmental and new academic challenges. The secondary curriculum focuses on the individual student's needs and finds ways to encourage academic as well as social and emotional growth. The exposure and goals of secondary school students' experience is a combination of conceptual development, skill acquisition, individual personal development and academic growth.

Children's academic excellence needs parental involvement as well as families and communities who take an active role in creating a caring educational environment. Within cultures and religions, family is known as the indispensable, smallest structural unit of human society. Family is the center of love where individual personality is formed, and values and traditions are passed on to new generations. As Pope Francis stated, "One could say, without exaggeration, that the family is the driving force of the world and of history." The concept of parental involvement between children and the school is a necessary one and can yield great rewards for all stakeholders. Parent engagement in almost any form produces measurable increase in the child's academic achievement.

From birth, you as parents are told that your involvement is the solution to your child's academic excellence, but is there a point where being involved becomes more of a hindrance than help? Yes. Even though, I will not judge any parenting styles, there are some actions that inhibit the next generation's success. Children of these parents live in constant fear and lack trust in any adults. Parents in this category claim they have done more than enough for their children and yet their children are still not pleased. As some people will say, "Do you want me to go and steal for you?" In response to the parent's emotions, children conclude it's their own bad behavior that brought bad luck to their family. Such unfavorable parent comments disrupts healthy child development, causing young people to grow up believing they will always be a disappointment to their parents.

Again, when children become teenagers, they are forced to listen to their parents' criticisms, adapt to problematic situations, put themselves in their parents' shoes, help, tolerate, and console. In all these cases, the teenagers have no right to speak their mind.

Children's academic excellence requires parents to continue demonstrating growing independence, model positive parent-child relationships and nurture such relationships over time. When parents need to share information with children, they should speak

Children's academic excellence requires parents to demonstrate positive relationships and nurture them over time.

respectfully. Parents do not need to talk down to their child.

Parents who desire academic excellence for their child will need to be calm, resourceful and use plenty of humor. These parents will offer capable, true adult and child role models with high moral standards. They will also make deliberate acts of engagement to stay in touch with the specific needs of the child. These acts are found to have a profound effect on academic achievement.

When parents say encouraging things long enough, confidence starts to become a part of the child's belief system. So true. And I wish I'd had this confidence instilled in me from an even younger age.

—DR. FRANCISCA ENIH
Texas, 2020

1 | ACADEMIC EXCELLENCE

WHAT IS ACADEMIC EXCELLENCE?

To every parent, academic excellence should represent a child's ability to perform, achieve, and be exceptionally good in school subjects. Today, academic excellence is narrowly confined to those who achieve high grades, but academic excellence requires more than just making good grades in school and participating in extra-curricular activities.

Society asks for the child's highest level of maturity in cognitive, affective domains and the ability to do something well and of service to human beings collectively. Parents can provide opportunities to accelerate growth. These children are going to be ready to demonstrate skills in self-directed learning, thinking, research and communication as evidenced by the projects and performances that reflect individuality and creativity—and are advanced in relation to children of similar age or environment.

Children who have academic excellence are able to produce products and performance of professional quality upon graduation. These children are able to work together with others as a group as well as work independently. They demonstrate self-awareness, self-management, responsible decision making, social awareness and relationship skills at home, school and in their community.

It is true that parents are teachers, guides, leaders, protectors and providers for their children, but you do not need celebrity status to be successful as a parent. Your success comes instead from your determination, hard work and ability to foresee or apply knowledge-based experiences to situations.

I didn't start out to become a parenting professional. In fact, I'm not very interested in parenting styles. It's just that there is a certain kind of parenting these days that confuses our children, therefore impeding their chances to develop into all-round citizens. This will not lead our children to a future that society demands of them.

> *Academically successful children demonstrate self-awareness, responsible decision making, social awareness and strong relationship skills.*

We should not spend a lot of time being overly concerned about parents who aren't involved enough in the lives of their kids. The issue of educating economically disadvantaged minority students has become the focus of federal legislation mandated in the No Child Left Behind Act (NCLB), partly because educating all children to their full potential is the right thing to do. Much attention has been given to the achievement of these students as compared to their white counterparts, said President George W. Bush. However, schools and school districts across the country are attempting to accomplish this task with seemingly little success.

At the other end of the spectrum, there is a lot of harm going on as well, where parents feel a child can't be successful unless the parent is protecting and preventing at every turn, hovering, micromanaging, and steering their child toward some small subset of colleges and careers.

As good God is my witness, in raising my three beautiful children I've had these inclinations myself. But the result of such parental behavior is that our children end up living a scheduled childhood. They are kept safe and sound at home, provided with nutritious food and water to foster their growth. Parents want to be sure children attend the best schools, are enrolled in the right classes at those best schools, and that they earn exceptional grades in the right classes in those best schools.

These parents are highly knowledgeable of college and society requirements from the children that include "the ability to do something well and of service to human beings collectively." Therefore, these parents are not just satisfied with acceptable grades... they want absolutely the highest scores. They want their children to earn honors, accolades and awards, to be the best at sports, activities, and leadership. These parents tell their children, "Don't just join a club, start a club, because colleges want to see that. And check the box for community service. Show the colleges you care about others."

Hence, parents need to help themselves to improve and embrace parenting styles that will not get in the way of their child's emotional development. We all know that success in education is vital for a child's future. Parental involvement can add colors to the children's performance at school and positively impact their diligence, seriousness and cleverness.

Achieving academic excellence is a process of both formal and informal education. Indeed, education is a limitless and unending process to be enjoyed for a lifetime. Informal education, in terms of this book, is the education at home that parents, grandparents, family or neighbors in the community provide. It usually occurs outside of a structured learning environment. Informal education helps to ensure student interest inside the regular classroom, and beyond. It is the regular conversation, the daily investigation, and magnification of the child's experience. Often there is an unbiased link to some enlarged plan, but not every time. Parents' goals for informal education are to provide children with the skills needed to eventually understand more complex material.

Parents need to understand that informal education will help their child increase prior knowledge and understanding of the world. Education helps children develop and own skills that make their lives more interesting and enjoyable. Both formal and informal education are necessary and help in their own unique ways.

Parental involvement should require engagement together with the child in the same activity. It's important that parents communicate with their children on a regular basis. These communications should be simple, truthful and encouraging. Tailor your regular communications through intentional counselling on what should be done or improved and what should be discouraged so that the ultimate success of your child can be achieved. This suggests that you must settle it in your hearts to be of great assistance to your children so their desires will be accomplished.

When parents get involved in their child's education, it should begin early in the process. Early communication, encouragement and counseling will have more effects and power. However, the greatest expected results come from parental involvement that works directly uninterrupted with children on the process of acquiring knowledge and skills through activities at home.

Parents whose children achieve academic excellence in school display the following distinguishing features or qualities:

1) The parent sets a stable daily family routine

How do they do it? These parents have established time and a quiet place for their children to use when they need to apply themselves to the acquisition of knowledge, such as reading, investigation or practice. The parents also use the schedule to assign responsibility for household chores. Everyday work around the house helps children to understand routine and to become able to solve problems in the future. The parent ensures that chores are done and are followed up. Also, the parent is firm about bedtime. This is because children and parents need about eight hours of sleep every night. These parents additionally ensure everyone has dinner together. They use dinner time to nourish their children, observe their physical, emotional and spiritual health, and for family informal and formal discussion after the meal.

2) At home, parents monitor out-of-school work, especially normal mental or bodily power, function, or process

How do they do it? These parents set limits on electronic media, particularly television, because of its potential impact. These parents are aware of how early media exposure affects children's cognitive development and academic excellence. Therefore, these parents set limits on screen time to maximize the positive and reduce the negative results. Unlike any other electronic media, these parents know the effect of screen time on children under age two.

Obviously, these parents are knowledgeable about educational television programs that are well-designed, age-appropriate, educational and beneficial to children under age two. However, preschoolers may better understand and learn from real-life experiences from their parents than from a video. Children who spend more than two hours on average per day watching television during their first few years of life may be associated with poorer cognitive development. On the other hand, television content is important for cognitive skills and academic achievement for children over two years of age.

> *Parents should communicate regularly with their children, providing simple, truthful encouragement.*

So true, early exposure to age-appropriate programs designed around formal education curriculum relates to cognitive and academic enhancement, while to the contrary, television programs that expose children to pure entertainment and violent content is associated with reduced cognitive development and minimized academic achievement.

Parents who are involved in their child's academic excellence will need to select well-created, age-appropriate programs and view those programs with their child to increase the positive effects of formal and informal media. The purpose is to inform policymakers, educators, parents, and others who work with young children about the impact of media, particularly television, on preschoolers, and what society can do to maximize the benefits and minimize the costs.

Strategies for checking up on children when parents are not home:

Parents of children with academic excellence are those who have advance plans for their children, be it a snow day, an unexpected business meeting, or babysitter plans that fell through. These all are reasons and times when you may need to leave your child home alone.

You will naturally worry the first time when leaving a child unsupervised. However, you can feel prepared and self-assured with some planning and a couple of trial runs. If handled well, staying home alone for children age ten or older can be a positive experience, giving them a sense of self-confidence and independence.

It's obvious that a five-year-old can't go it alone, but most 16-year-olds can. So, I will focus on those school-aged children in between. This action requires our personal assessments and observations of what your child knows. It can be hard to discern when kids are ready to handle being home alone because milestones of childhood development, maturity and awareness do not happen at the same time. Again, open communications will help to find out your child's feelings about staying at home alone for few hours of the day. Most children are confident that they will be good on their own long before parents feel okay with it. However, some older children may be scared to stay home alone even when the parents are confident they will do an outstanding job.

More points to consider before you allow your child to stay at home alone:

Understand the neighborhood in which you live and plan to leave your children. This includes talking to neighbors, especially on neighborhood night out. You can go online to check local crime rates or if there are pedophiles who live nearby. Neighborhood police department will always share information about your residential area. Your plans will be different if you reside on a busy street with lots of traffic versus a quiet cul-de-sac. Also, ensure that you have acquaintances nearby whom you know and trust will help your children in case of emergency. Please do not leave your child to strangers. Ensure the child knows to stay away from strangers.

Besides your location and friends, parents need to ensure the child is responsible to handle different situations like starting and completing homework, household chores, listening, following directions or rules, accepting "no," respecting and trying their best. It's important for your child to understand and follow safety measures and to know simple first-aid.

Even though we may be certain our children have the development or ability, it will be wise to stage a home-alone trial prior to the big day by letting the child stay home for thirty minutes or more, but less than sixty minutes, while the parent remains nearby and quickly reachable. Children like feedback, so discuss with your child how it went when you return and share insights or skills that you might want to change or learn for the next time.

Additionally, parents should teach children how and when to dial 911, to know their home address information, to lock and unlock doors, and how to operate the home security system if necessary. Children need to be able to work the house phone or cellphone, turn lights on and off, and operate the microwave oven. Parents should also teach children what to do in case of a small fire in the kitchen, when smoke alarms go off, if there is a tornado or severe weather, when a stranger comes to the door or someone calls for a parent who isn't at home, and when there's a power outage and flashlights are needed. Parents of academic excellence should always discuss emergency scenarios, like what to do if the child smells smoke, or an unknown "uncle" knocks at the door or a stranger asks for the parent while you are not at home.

After preparations are completed and you are confident your child is ready to stay home alone, here are procedures that can make it simple for the family.

Create a timetable for phone calls, when either you will call home, or the child will call you. Also create a list of family friends your child can call along with things your children can do when alone and bored.

Implement specific rules and ensure the child knows and understands them. Specifically address rules about having friends over in the house while parents are not there, and rooms of the house that are not for children or friends, screen time and types of programs, internet and computer rules. Kitchen appliances and knives should be made off-limits. Children should also get along with siblings and refrain from telling strangers about being home alone.

Parents should make sure the house has everyday goods and emergency supplies, including healthy foods for snacking. If the child takes medications, leave only the exact dose out for your child, keeping medicine bottles out of reach to avoid accidental overdose—especially by younger siblings in the household.

Parents of academic excellence ensure that their home is childproof. They secure hazardous chemicals. Keep alcohol, prescription medicines, and even over-the-counter medicines like sleeping pills and cough medicines out of reach. If you own a gun, make sure it is unloaded, stored separately from ammunition, and locked up safely. Also store things like tobacco, car keys, lighters and matches away from children. If possible, provide a friendly pet, like a hamster, to keep them company.

Optimize Your 15 Minutes a Day
so that you and your child can
Win the Day... Everyday!

Visit 15MinutesADayBook.com/Win

---

2 | PARENTAL INVOLVEMENT

Parents of children and adolescents (ages 5–14) looking for academic excellence arrange for after-school activities and supervised care that increase engaged learning opportunities. Some ideal activities include sports, piano lessons, religious classes, and scout troops. It is not advisable to leave your child unattended at public libraries, in subway stations or community shops. Instead look for programs after school and on weekends and summer break that are not only educationally enriching but keep children and adolescents safe from drug and alcohol use, and sexual activity. Make your child a partner in the decision-making and you will also encourage their healthy emotional development.

Be aware that your children are watching you. Be consistent, every moment, ensuring that your child acquires the desired knowledge and skills not only in education settings, but by observing your actions as a role model. You are always training your child to follow directions and obey rules, pay attention, and have a code of behavior. Use positive praise for good effort rather than results, and admonish to correct misconduct.

Understand the importance of self-control. Model for your child the value of effort and endurance. Teach your children "sweat then sweet." Do not criticize or judge, because nobody likes being told what is good or what is bad. Use positive praise to promote further development or advancement of an outcome that will be helpful to your children.

Teach the importance of working for something you believe in. Children need to learn to set goals and work hard to achieve them, which leads to happiness, success and makes you wholesome. Hard work requires both physical and mental exertion. Demonstrate to your child that mindset and success accompany hard work.

Encourage "sweat" before "sweet."

Parents who want academic excellence will make a point to develop character and age-appropriate situations and solutions to everyday problems when speaking to children. Use promising words to inspire more attention to details. Nurture the child to participate and engage cognitively, physically and emotionally to improve communication. Encourage and model interaction, remembering that learning and communication come together. Merge stories to use all the senses, developing learning opportunities that engage mental processes that involve the child's emotional, social, cognitive and physical needs.

Communicate effectively with your child to build self-confidence. When children are confident, they not only learn better, they want to learn more. It also helps them stay focused and increases their communication skills. Use this stronger communication to create awareness that the child is listened to, sheltered and safe from danger. This will increase their sense of trust in family, community and happiness about their existence. When possible, use visual aids and model the thinking you would like your child to emulate. Use positive models to demonstrate action you want them to take (such as "giving is from the heart, not from abundance," "sharing is caring") to strengthen positive action and thought.

From time to time you should encourage children to participate in decision making. This provides exposure for children to strengthen independence, and to understand that their contributions can be essential to family, neighbors, community and society. Meanwhile, monitor and encourage children to express their strengths and solutions—and not only their problems. They should also be encouraged to think and act both locally and globally. While teaching them to develop their own communication, they can be nurtured to develop values, morals and principles of equality, fairness and respect for others. Children can become models and ambassadors to their younger peers when they are encouraged to think and act "outside the box" in non-stereotypical, creative ways.

Parent involvement in your child's education requires sacrificing your time, comfort, leisure and pleasure in order to help your child navigate the way to success in their education. The cost may seem sacrificial but the glory of the success to come, and the joy it will bring to the family, will outweigh the sacrifice.

We as parents should correct our children with love. A parent is not always silent but speaks and encourages, and sometimes scolds, with delicacy and vigor to help children mature in the right direction—but with love and in private. Make every effort to help your child to turn from false paths. Ensure they are calm and never seeking perfection out of vexation. Instead, your message should be that you are there to help. Parental involvement in the child's academic life is highly recommended for all ages, but especially for teenagers who may have to be taught to obey rules with a goal of harmony and understanding.

Mothers have special gifts to help with the education, intellect, manner of speech and style of dress that will promote social mobility in a society. Women are the ones who have usually been tasked with overseeing homework and family. This will be true of both single and married women. For example, in a typical weekday, a mother may leave the office early to pick up children from school, but then be worn out and lacking energy to listen to their partner while fixing dinner later that night. Mothers are often expected to care for and nurture others, but it comes at a cost. There is more pressure on mothers to continue to promote and protect their family, managing relationships within both the family and the community.

Therefore, a mother's education will be used as a measure of a family's wealth and success. Social status is reflected by way of not only education but belief systems that translate into actions. Parents use their resources to guide these actions and represent their value of academic excellence.

The effects of a mother's level of education and other attributes are different for each type of involvement. It is important to know that the mother's level of education, both formal and informal, is one of the main factors associated with parent involvement in a child's education. If mothers know the advantage of education for their children, and they have the resources, their beliefs are then translated into action.

Fathers may value education but in practice they are less likely to use hands-on direct involvement in the child's education, thus their values may not be impressed. It is mothers who most frequently have the routine role of caregiver for the family. So, when mothers are highly accomplished, and maintain the role of caregiver, they can directly transfer their wealth of knowledge to their children. Mothers with higher levels of education are in a better position to not only make decisions about their child's education, but also to give them the resources to do so.

The work of family caregiving is in the interlinking of domestic expertise and public institutions. Mothers are the target of policy ideas to improve home-and-school relationships, while the redistribution of argument for education away from schools and toward parents has disproportionately increased the workload of women in relation to that of their male counterparts.

Recently a mother's domestic labor includes an extension rather than a separation of their paid work from work that supports their children's education. This means that a mother's paid work can change the nature of their involvement in the child's education.

Changes in economy have influenced middle-class mothers. They are at the front line of social reproduction, heavily invested in terms of time and mental and emotional labor. Mothers have a different relationship to the generation of cultural capital, and concomitantly, social class than fathers. It is mothers who are making cultural capital work for their children. Mothers, not fathers, will be the agents of social class reproduction. Mothers work to bridge the gap between family social class and children's academic performance in the classroom. Maternal practices will determine the class much more than materiality. The family class is seen not only in mothers' activities in support of children's schooling, but also in the mother's attitudes, assumptions and levels of entitlement in relation to children's academic achievement.

Mothers are the first teacher of their children, and their work as parents can be more important than any they perform in the labor market to enhance their family's social position and the class differences that buttress it. Mothers are aware of class practices and its existence in the 21st century. Class processes within families are components that connect the businesses of the society marketplace. Mothers' work is necessary, and it has a relationship with children's academic achievement and education systems allows for an understanding of mothers' work as social propagation in action.

Women are typically the ones tasked with overseeing homework and the family.

In some societies in which market forces are from mothers "acting in their children's best interests" it means middle-class mothers are at the same time acting against the interests of children from less privileged mothers. This is not to point fingers at middle-class mothers; however, we need to see all mothers as possessed in educational markets which operate on the selfish beliefs of "to her who has yet more shall be given."

Educational success becomes a function of social, cultural and material advantages in which mothers' caring within the family is transmuted by the operations of the wider marketplace to serve its competitive, self-interested individualistic ethos. Mothers' daily routines, maintenance, training and emotional work supports the workings of educational markets contributing to a civilization of winners and losers within which one child's academic success is at the expense of another child's failure.

Optimize Your 15 Minutes a Day
so that you and your child can
Win the Day… Everyday!

Visit 15MinutesADayBook.com/Win

---

3 | Conducive Atmosphere for Educational Success

Every parent will need to enhance the current home atmosphere to help their children succeed in the 21st century, because those same children will work in jobs that don't currently exist right now. We need to examine what skills are needed and which activities will ensure students will be adequately prepared.

As we explore the best possible environment for physical and mental development, we have learned that children need their parents' compliments for their efforts—not for their results. Through words of encouragement and praise, it demonstrates the child's value.

Academic excellence is built on a relationship between the child and parent that is not reliant on material goods. Depending on family income and number of children in the household, there are only so many possessions parents can provide. Therefore, it is important to focus on the fundamental elements that enhance potential.

Compliment your child's efforts, not the results.

Please create time to spend with your child. Success and wealth mean little without quality time, relationships and experiences. When my grandmother was alive, I remember her saying, "Have good manners. Being respectful is better than silver or good." Let us teach our children how to be more independent and self-sufficient, while sharing the value of integrity.

Help your children learn to accept positive or negative feedback and apply it, speak up for themselves, know their responsibilities and know their routine. My grandmother's lessons made me understand the importance of helping those less fortunate, and recognizing actions that led to corruption and destruction to the community.

While you as a parent invest so much time and interest to increase your child's knowledge and success in the "three R's"—reading, writing and arithmetic achievement—remember the additional importance of social and creative skills. These include adaptability, communication, creativity, curiosity, collaboration, flexible, critical thinking and leadership. These latter skills complement the intelligent quotient skills and build positive outcomes. Our children are born with these gifts, but we can also foster and further develop them.

Help your children learn to speak up for themselves.

The goal is to create an atmosphere at home for academic excellence where your children learn to increase their self-awareness and impulse control early in life. In addition, it's important to encourage children to use their natural talents and gifts to create and build—or dismantle something—they are interested in. You can help children use the tools needed to build or disassemble in a safe space. The ideal location to learn such skills will be at home, before children leave for college or employment.

While our school system educates and engages children competitively, society demands that parents allow kids to be kids, giving them the opportunity to explore and learn from outside experiences. Hence, you should remember that children learn by imitation—including the behavior, skills and attitude of their peers, parents, teachers, other caregivers, and everyone in their immediate living environment. Be aware that you are your child's earliest role model.

Skills and conducive atmosphere our children need to succeed

Parents are the child's first teacher and the home is their first classroom. We generate the most success and genuine excitement when we let the child's curiosity drive. Allow children to ask questions, value those questions, and answer encouragingly. Incorporate a variety of learning experiences—stories and hands-on activities—that are age-appropriate, with a diversity of gender, socio-economic status, culture and other opportunities.

Skills like creativity, curiosity, communication, collaboration, critical thinking, leadership, adaptability and social skills are becoming popular not only in the classroom, but in the workforce. Beyond traditional IQ elements of reading, writing, arithmetic, these skills enable children to translate facts and figures into practical information. They are non-cognitive skills and key to future success.

Therefore, your home and setting will include the elements for fostering communication, collaboration, leadership, critical thinking, adaptability, creativity and social skills.

Allow children to make mistakes. Perfection is not the goal, but rather to learn and adapt. It is wonderful to observe them growing in skills, knowledge, and vision. This is much easier to learn at a young age!

Your child will need this balance between traditional intelligence (IQ—reading, writing, arithmetic), and emotional intelligence (EI—self-control, self-awareness, the ability to work independently and to maintain impulse control). Other EI skills you can help your child develop include communication, collaboration, teamwork, active listening, empathy, and playing well with others. You can encourage your child to participate in exploration, asking questions about new items and actions, which develops curiosity and inquisitiveness.

Model confident communication, celebrate your child's strengths, acknowledge psychological vulnerability, and intervene when needed. Model perseverance. Set goals, spring into action, and encourage children to "reach for the stars." Demonstrate that obstacles are merely roadblocks to overcome. When your child takes appropriate action, give rewards for intrinsic and extrinsic motivation. Consider praising your child's innovation, imagination, and out-of-the-box thinking.

It is important for you to understand that your child is not only listening to what you say, but also watching what you do. In most situations, for better or worse, you serve as the primary role model, setting examples through daily interaction with other family members, neighbors and friends in the community. Therefore, you have a responsibility to behave in a way your child will admire. Control your temper, and act with fairness, justice, kindness, love, and tolerance.

Parents play an especially critical role in communicating principles and beliefs. Being consistent is what's most important. When children feel attractive and valued, they are more likely to create strong bonds with a wonderful spouse, which leads to a happy life.

> You have a responsibility to behave in a way your child will admire.

Read to your child starting from the moment they're born. Children from homes where reading is treasured enter school with an exponentially larger vocabulary, as well as exposure to a wider variety of cultures and beliefs.

Other activities that increase children's emotional intelligence skills include museum visits, concert attendance, and travel. These can connect material they are learning in school to a broader range of intellectual and cultural benefits.

Be cautious not to push too far, however. Remember to give your child freedom for experiential learning. During these activities, they learn through trial and error, eventually succeeding. Let children use their common sense. Compliment them, play with them and celebrate with them. Failure should not be anxiety inducing, but rather viewed as an opportunity for growth and continued learning.

The core personality of your child is very much influenced by experiences with you. I still hear my parents' voices in my head when I am doing something I know my mother would be upset about. It's been a lot of years. But that voice is still there. Make sure the voice your child remembers is one of support and encouragement.

Optimize Your 15 Minutes a Day
so that you and your child can
Win the Day... Everyday!

Visit 15MinutesADayBook.com/Win

---

4 | PARENTAL MORAL SUPPORT

What does moral support mean to our children?

When it comes to raising children of academic excellence, moral support is the assistance we give our children under normal circumstances without getting directly involved in their activities.

You may be anxious to find the best after-school program or daycare, but the truth of the matter is that your child needs you to spend time with them. Consider engaging in household activities as well as playing games. A child might spend one hour twice a week baking with you, or two hours a week assembling a jigsaw puzzle in a race. Spend more time on a regular basis.

When I was still young and in school, we used to have dinner together. Every day our parents would ask us what we failed at that day. We would laugh about it, but through this experience, our parents taught us that failure was not really a catastrophe. It was just an experience. It is good to try and fail. To my parents, a true failure would have been not to try at all because of fear.

Strive to create an atmosphere of no shame, and no belittling—just love and kindness. You do not want your child to wish you would just leave them alone. Neither do you want your child to be anxious that you might look at them with fear or judgment. When one fault is detected, children proceed to list them all... as they imagine what a scornful parent might be criticizing.

Parental moral support does not have to take a major toll on your time and energy. Here are some starting methods.

Develop a routine schedule of activities besides those oriented around school subjects. These can include house cleaning, have children make their own beds in the morning, laundry, taking out the trash, washing dishes, making simple meals like sandwiches, and using the microwave oven. If children learn to do chores at a young age, they will learn to follow directions joyfully and also become more responsible decision makers and dedicated adults later in life. Practice fosters independence. Do not feel the need to relieve or exempt your child from chores.

Parents of academic excellence teach their children simple social skills and manners. Children should learn when to say hello, excuse themselves, say good morning, and use simple table manners such as how to hold a fork and knife. These experiences and skills help build healthy and rewarding relationships with a child's peers, allow them to better understand their friends' feelings, and learn to independently resolve their own problems. The results of good social skills allow children to communicate effectively, collaborate with others, attend and earn a college degree and hold a full-time job. On the other hand, children with poor social skills lack cooperation with their peers, have trouble understanding others' feelings, and suffer from an increased chance of getting in trouble with the law, binge drinking and unemployment.

Develop high expectations for your child. Coach positively rather than using words of discouragement. Set the stage for your child to be successful, conveying your expectations in ways that will not be considered intrusive or controlling. Recognize the importance of college attendance to your child's future, and work together with your child to reach this goal, regardless of socio-economic status or income. Even though my parents had eleven children, our father worked two jobs while our mother was a petty trader. Both encouraged us to continue our education beyond secondary school. In my family's case, everyone graduated from college except my deceased sister.

Provide clear descriptions of the desirable outcomes, and explain what can happen if they do not take school seriously. Parents need to use encouraging words, such as "You are awesome!" "You're the smart one!" at various points throughout the child's life. These phrases will be important to motivate children to succeed academically, as well as increasing their sense of family responsibility.

We use moral lessons to teach our children. Sometimes they might believe life could be better without their parents or siblings. A good example was my younger sister, Helen, who used to be very defiant. She would not help with chores because she thought we had too many people in the house to cook for and clean up after. Our parents developed a routine schedule for us to cook and do dishes on a daily basis, and to mop the entire house on Saturdays. Also, children would do laundry on Saturdays and iron uniforms and clothes. On

Sundays we attended mass and served as greeters, altar boys, ushers, or choir members.

Helen was sixteen then. Her dream was to be at home with fewer children, less headaches, left alone and with less housework. On May 26, 1984, our Aunty got married, and Helen requested to stay home with me and our brother so that she could finish her school and housework. But Helen did not cooperate with us at home. She had planned to enjoy the weekend with her friends. On that Saturday, she woke up late, ate, then left the house with her assignments and housework undone. Later, in the afternoon, we learned Helen was involved in a car accident.

We rushed to see her at the hospital. When our parents returned that evening, Helen was discharged. We did not finish our assigned weekend routine. Everyone was more concerned about Helen's health. Her chores had to be reassigned and shared by her siblings. Mother cooked and encouraged us to help braid Helen's hair, while our father took her to the family doctor for thorough check-ups.

> *Moral support means encouraging the presence of God in others—even from those whom we least expect.*

That week, the homily at our church was about moral support. Moral support is also one of the great virtues of the Bible. The ancients believed that one should support each person as though one were welcoming God himself. Jesus expresses this virtue by saying, "Whoever receives you receives me, and whoever receives me receives the one who sent me." Moral support is much more than just being a good host at a dinner party. Moral support means encouraging the presence of God in others, usually in those whom we least expect.

Sometimes we get so self-absorbed in our cares that we miss the presence of the Lord as he stands right before us in our family or as he knocks on the door of our homes and lives through other people. We often miss the presence of God in others because we have preconceived notions of how this presence should be. The virtue of moral support is recognizing the presence of God in others and nourishing it. When we practice this virtue, then the stranger among us is no longer a stranger, but a member of the family, welcomed to enjoy a room in our house and lives. Let us pray for an openness to God's presence in ways we least expect.

Parents need to help children to take a close look at daily activities and encourage them to stay focused more on caring for each other than caring for things. Teach your children that real love does not expect a payback.

After Helen recovered, she was happy to become part of the family since everyone had helped her to heal and our parents forgave her. She admitted that she had lied and that she had come to recognize the essence of family support.

Another stellar example of the power of moral support came just two years ago. As a middle school Special Education teacher and coordinator for field trips and activities, I had the opportunity to chaperone our school district's Special Olympics. The event included students from elementary through high school competing in basketball, tennis, soccer, and track and field, as well as flag football for high schoolers, and was held at Butler Stadium in Houston.

During that event, my students competed in several events. The students were all disabled in some way: autism, speech and language impairments, traumatic brain injury, intellectual disabilities, emotional disturbance, and Down syndrome. Each lined up for the start of the 100-yard dash. At the sound of the starter's whistle, all got off well, except one female student who tripped over her own feet, tumbled to the ground, scraped her arm, and began to cry.

When other students heard her cry, the other five all slowly stopped, turned around and went back to where the fallen girl lay. One boy with Down syndrome bent down and kissed her injured arm. "This will make it better," he said. Then all six children and some parents held hands and walked together to the finish line. On that day everyone at the event stood speechless as they had the privilege to witness love and moral support from parents, teachers and other students.

Parental moral support at home increases children's academic excellence and comes out as an extension of the overall parenting style. These parents' messages are always positive and encouraging. They believe with all their heart that young people can solve big problems and so they ensure that they communicate confidence to their children.

The way you communicate ideas to your child has a significant factor in molding their character and self-confidence. Your dream is to raise children who are happy, healthy and confident. Our society needs cheerful humans and it is possible to raise these children in every home today. As a parent of three amazing children and grandparent of beautiful boy and a girl, I have come to realize there are sure ways to interact with our children to increase their success in life.

Set limits for your child. Our society has rules and structure for everyone. Parents need to establish communication, discipline, and obedience for their children. Kids need their parents to provide a set of guidelines so they have some structure in their lives, and know what to expect. This gives them consistency.

Society needs cheerful humans!

Parental moral support includes helping your child by modeling and communicating the behavior that you want to see in them. Avoid put-downs and negative phrases, instead focusing on the positive. For example, if a child spills food or a drink ask, "The food spilled on the floor. What should we do?" If the child is in a distressing situation say, "I see that you are upset. How can I help?"

One easy way to build confidence daily is to ask children to discuss at least three situations in which they felt proud of themselves. You can do this at the dinner table, or at bedtime. While your child is discussing the day, never criticize. Always tell them how wonderful they are. Always tell them how good and smart they are. Note some adults are still struggling with self-esteem issues, and this could be because they were never complimented when they were young. Some were always criticized but now they have healed and are able to help others in society. We need to raise confident children by giving them positive feedback.

If you observe that your child has interest in painting or sketching, support that gift with art supplies. It need not be expensive. Then let the child make his own decisions on what he wants to create or express. You may find art to be an incredible way for the child to express himself, especially when he is young and life experiences are still so raw and new. Encourage the creativity by commenting how you admire the concrete accomplishment they made, trying not to exaggerate.

Another way you can foster confidence and independence is by letting the child decide on little things like which haircut they want, or which pieces of clothing to wear.

Children subconsciously need guidance and rules in order to build more confidence. When we as parents help our children by doing different tasks with them on a daily basis, these actions helps them feel proud of themselves because they do such wonderful creative projects.

Moral support plays a main role in bonding with children. When your child is upset, remember never to laugh at them. It's not a good way of approaching the problem. Instead, talk to the child in a respectful manner and take this to heart—you can shine more positivity into your children's lives.

Remember that the time spent with your children should make them happy and more productive. You are their earliest role model, but you can also provide them with good books and surround them with people who care.

However, in spite of all the good you are doing, children will often fight with siblings, and sometimes they may not listen... but they do hear your voice, and it will remain in their head for years to come. Your parental moral support will encourage them to set goals, take consistent action to achieve them, and feel loved and supported in every way.

Optimize Your 15 Minutes a Day
so that you and your child can
Win the Day... Everyday!

Visit 15MinutesADayBook.com/Win

5 | MONITORING AND ASSISTING WITH SCHOOL ASSIGNMENTS

When it comes to academic excellence at school, a parent's role is important in motoring and assisting children in doing their assignments. The parent's actions are as simple as having base knowledge and providing a little support and direction. Your help at home can integrate and extend the learning of the day. Therefore, supporting your child at home must be made into a fun experience and not a chore, especially at an early age. Examples could include sharing a storybook, or helping children write their name, or counting their toys to practice numbers.

When helping with homework, it is not the time to showcase all you know on the topic. Instead, be supportive by explaining critical thinking problems, encouraging children where to look for answers, or just providing nutritious snacks when it's time for a break. Sometimes, while helping children with homework, you might even learn a thing or two.

Monitoring our children's academic excellence requires willingness, flexibility, motivation and sometimes self-sacrifice. The starting point is to communicate the importance of homework. Request the assignments every day immediately when your child enters the home. When you do this on a day-to-day basis, your child will be more likely to listen, obey and complete it.

Remind children that the skills they acquire today will help them in the future. For example, tell your would-be actress daughter that she won't be able to memorize her lines if she's not a stellar reader. For the athletic child the rule should be "no pass, no play!"

The next step is to let your child develop some ownership about when to do the homework assignments. Be accessible to answer questions or help with problems, but do not make homework time even more painful by hovering over the child or judging everything they do.

Eliminate distractions, even if that means you can't watch television or chat on the phone during homework time. While your children are working, consider doing some "homework" of your own, like paying bills or reading a trade journal. This will reinforce the whole impression of homework and it will seem less unfair.

Be generous with praise, especially with elementary children. Give kids a thumbs up, sticker, or verbal praise for simply doing the homework without complaining. When homework is done consistently, consider a larger reward like clothing, a video game, a family trip to a park, or permission to go to a concert or party they're dying to attend.

Set up occasional study dates with friends for students in secondary grade level. Each student's work should be their own, but studying with a friend can make the process more fun. Just check with the teacher to make sure working in a group is allowed.

If nothing is working, try reverse psychology. Sometime parents should completely stop nudging, and let their children discover the consequences of not doing homework. Then be welcoming when they come crawling back. If it's always a fight, that's not good for either of you.

To promote success at school, take an active interest in the child's homework. It can give your child a feeling of approval, knowing that what they do is important to you. I have heard some parents say, "School should stay at school," because it can be stressful balancing homework on top of a forty-hour work schedule.

Here are some simple tips, tools and solutions for stress-free homework:

First, give children something to look forward to after completing their homework.

Establish and communicate a designated time to start homework.

- Right after school
- After about a half-hour break
- Before dinner
- After dinner
- Before bedtime

Younger kids really need to start homework after school. Usually about a half-hour break is a good maximum amount of time. Establish the expectation that they get started then… whether you're a working parent or meeting them at the bus. When your young child comes home, take that half-hour break then start the homework routine.

Secondary school children will want to push the time. These higher-grade level children want to start later. However, you should help your child consider starting homework before dinner.

Routine is important, and it does not matter the specific time or location in the home. A good homework station does not have to be just one spot, but it is important to have a desk or somewhere in the bedroom, home office, or dining room where children will be productive. Certainly, the place should be distraction free.

If your child seems to be taking too long to complete homework assignments, or feels overwhelmed every night, consult with the teacher. Your child's teachers do not know what goes on in the home with the children. It can be as simple as sending an email or placing a phone call. Say, "I have noticed that this homework is taking my child far longer than normal and causing frustration."

The rule of time length is generally ten minutes of homework per grade level. Hence a first-grade should have ten minutes while a fifth-grade should expect fifty minutes. If your find that your child is taking much more time, then let the teacher know.

The use of television, video games, music in the background, or cell phones during homework time are big distractions and should be avoided. The essence of homework is to practice, improve and keep learning so that knowledge moves into long-term memory. Therefore, children need a conducive environment without music in the background when studying for a test.

When your child reaches secondary school, work out a deal when it comes to cell phone use. The phone should really be in another part of the room, or in a different room altogether during homework time. So maybe they should work on their homework for twenty or thirty minutes and then they can go check their messages and send a quick text… but then it's back to homework.

When you notice repeating or repetitive problems with you child in relation to schoolwork, don't wait until parent-teacher conferences in November. Especially if your child has had difficulty in the past, send a welcome email at the beginning of the year just to introduce yourself. Tell the teacher about any issues that your child has struggled with in the past, and let the teacher know you are on their side. You want to support the teacher and be part of the team. Let that person know that educating your child means a lot to you and that you want good advice.

Nowadays, monitoring our children's use of technology is essential. You need to talk with them about the various technologies, and you will also need to check their contacts over time because you want to raise great digital citizens. Take responsibility for your children's use of various devices. Set limits and monitor usage, instructing and encouraging positive behavior.

You are not only responsible for food, clothing, shelter and education; you need to be responsible for monitoring computer, tablet and cell phone use. If you are not checking your child's Roblox, Minecraft, Snapchat or Instagram, then somebody else will be. Is that what you want?

Keep in mind that an average sixth-grade student has an expensive cell phone or technology device. This is like giving your child the keys to a brand-new Mercedes, Lamborghini, or Bentley and saying, "Sweetheart, you can go cruise to your choice of places—California, Florida, or Vegas. And when you come back, Mommy and Daddy will fill that tank up and you can just go again. Just don't tell us if you did anything wrong." You never would do that, would you?

Talk to your child about their contacts and how to make a simple verification for safety before sharing personal information. Teach them to ask for the person's first and last name, where they live, the school they attend, and their phone number. For example, your son Cameron can verify that Sabrina is in his mathematics class, she lives in southwest Houston. and her phone number is (000) 000-0000. Teach your children that if they cannot verify this information yourself, especially for online friends, then that contact is probably a liar.

Remember, to use positive communication. Do not threaten with words like "You will be grounded," "Your phone will be taken away," or "The hinges of your bedroom door will come off." Since you bought the technology and gave it to your child, then you are ultimately responsible!

Sit down with the child and have that positive technology talk. Let them know you will check the device routinely, and also monitor it remotely, as well as checking any social media accounts. Encourage them to reach out to you if something bad happens. For example, you might say, "If you feel like someone is making you do something you do not want to do, or someone is making you feel bad about yourself, please come to me. There will be no consequences. Your phone will not be taken away. You won't be grounded." That gives children the golden ticket. This golden ticket agreement talk will promote their safety and open communication with you.

If you notice your child acting strange or worried, yet they will not engage with you in conversation about it, especially if the situation escalates, you may want to gain access to your child's phone and various accounts so you can look for red flags.

Fostering academic excellence includes being able to meet your child's teachers. Become involved and ask about homework policies. Needed school supplies include paper, pen, pencil, crayon, glue, scissors, calculator, and a chair and table.

You may have to encourage children on heavy homework nights or test study nights. For older children, remind them to take a break every hour, and to divide the homework into manageable chunks. Provide water and healthy snacks during breaks, and remove distractions like the television, loud music, and others chatting on the phone. However, if children have specific questions about the assignment, a phone call to a classmate can be helpful.

"Practice makes perfect" is an old saying, but children need to complete their own work. Parents should only make suggestions and help with directions. Allow your child to make mistakes. That is how everyone learns.

Be available for questions and concerns, motivating and monitoring by verifying assignments, quizzes and test preparation, completion and due dates. Be a role model as well; let children see you reading a book, thinking out loud, and sticking to a plan. One example is making and following a family budget. Children learn faster when they see you modeling good behavior.

Above all, show love to children by rewarding and praising their efforts. Celebrate academic achievements and share the results with other relatives. Post comments like "Great job" on the refrigerator. Show your love and support!

Parents of academic excellence ensure their children have regular school attendance. Every class session builds on the previous lesson, so if a child misses one lesson, it creates a gap in their learning. When absences occur, make sure to ask for any homework given, and ensure your child completes it before returning to school.

Make sure your student turns in all the homework. This teaches children responsibility, and it also helps the teacher pinpoint where students are facing difficulty. it is essential that all homework be completed by the child and turned in on time. Encourage the child with praise and reward. Your child's self-esteem is important to their future success.

Children need to believe they're succeeding, and that they *can* succeed. This depends largely on what you as a parent have communicated to them. Avoid multi-tasking while you help your child with homework. Especially do not watch television or listen to music. This approach does not work. Logically children can only give their full attention to one thing at a time.

Encourage reading. A good reading habit is a pillar for success in school and throughout life. Read with your children from a young age. When they get older, encourage them to read to you, and later to read on their own. Allow them to choose books for themselves, and always try to set a good example by reading in their company. Make reading a fun thing you do together.

Most of all, refrain from adding extra pressure on your child to succeed. This can stress out your adolescent's mental and physical health. Certainly children will have many experiences they must learn to cope with, from school to extracurriculars. These can all lead to an increase in mental health issues, but be sure you are not adding undo pressure.

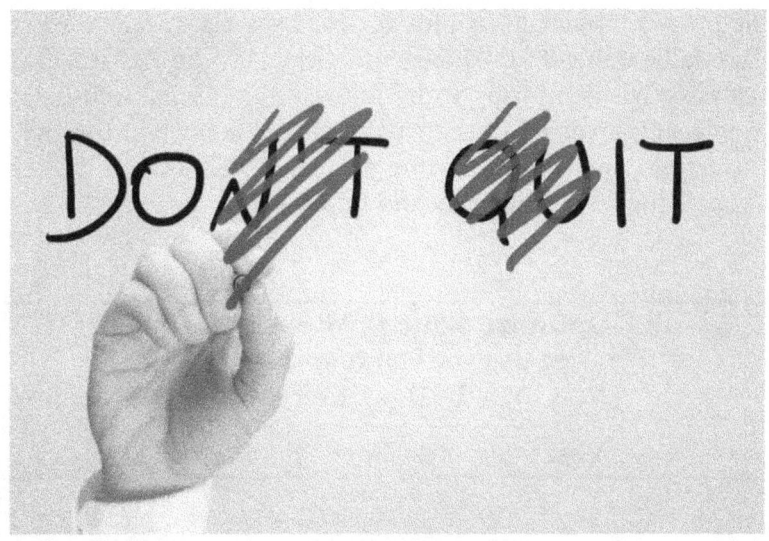

You are there to assist your child, not hover or do everything for them. Some parents today think that if they shelter their children, the kids will not make any mistakes… but it is most likely that they will. Parents who are over involved are just as harmful as parents who are not involved enough. It is true that you do not want your child to fail or make the same mistakes you did, but failing also allows a child to prosper and learn more than when they succeed. Parents of successful children are not wrapped up in grades or extracurriculars, but they are worried about how their children are doing.

Do not forget to ask older children about how they are feeling regarding stress. Let children learn from their childhood memories of difficult situations. This is beneficial to the overall success of the child and who they will become over time. Millionaires didn't wake up one morning and say they wanted to become a millionaire. They made mistakes and they learned from those outcomes. Sometimes they were not even capable of jumping one hurdle, but they became better people because of it. Help your child to continue to aim for a purpose, to persevere and have the drive to succeed.

Mental health will significantly affect your children as they age. An adolescent's potential decreases significantly when mentally unhealthy. Make sure they stay on the road to success, by monitoring your children's emotional well-being and being involved in their lives. Give guidance in the right direction, and allow children to make their own mistakes. That is how they will learn and improve.

Optimize Your 15 Minutes a Day
so that you and your child can
Win the Day... Everyday!

Visit 15MinutesADayBook.com/Win

---

6 | Advocating for Your Child at School

It is every parent's dream to raise children who are successful and productive citizens in the community and in society. Advocating for your children means empowering them with public support and making recommendations for policy changes when necessary. The impact of the above will give children a voice and a say in whatever situation they find themselves. It's about helping them to not have to stand alone.

For instance, if your child or relative has been mistreated, you will need outside help from someone who is objective about the matter. Sometimes it's about bullying. Sometimes it's physical abuse. The issues will vary dramatically. As an immigrant to the United States, I did not always get fair treatment. Instead of complaining pointlessly, I immediately started to write and call business phone numbers for help. When someone is in pain, this should not be allowed to continue. You deserve so much better. And your children deserve better. In most cases the person at the other end of the line will listen to you. Find someone to support you and your child in whatever issue has occurred. Often when we seek out help, it's because something dreadful has happened.

We all need help to have our voices heard. Sometimes, we are unable to say how we feel about things and what we want to happen. We need advocacy to provide the connection. This is even truer for children.

Just being there beside your child will make their school assignments less frightening and daunting. Knowing that they can say or ask you anything means more than any material possession. Due to age and inexperience, children need their parents to help them articulate their problem, to speak on their behalf, and to lead them through the process. It is important that everyone who needs an advocate gets one. You and your child deserve to have your voices heard.

TIPS FOR SUCCESSFUL ADVOCACY

You will be called to advocate for your child at some point when a complaint or deficiency is observed. As a parent you want your child to succeed in school. One way you can stay informed about your child's progress is to be involved in classroom and school activities. Keep in regular contact with your child's teachers through email and/or phone calls and check the website for homework assignments, study guides and other resources that will help your child succeed. Staying informed is step one of successful advocacy for your child.

An excellent resource to stay in touch is the Parent Portal where you can find information about your child's attendance, discipline, course links, and class schedules as well as email addresses for teachers. The attendance page shows the days of activity and a summary of attendance for each absence type. The grade page lists the most recent scores earned by your child, and for high school students, the graduation requirements page notes credits earned and the number of credits currently being attempted.

Staying informed is step one of successful advocacy for your child.

It is very important that you build positive relationships with your child's teachers, administrators, guidance counselors, coaches and other school staff members. These folks provide information about their classroom expectations to all parents at the beginning of the semester or school year. These expectations are also posted on teacher websites. Back-to-school nights are an excellent way to meet your child's teachers and to hear about their expectations.

Advocacy, at its core, is a deeply embedded sense of purpose. It is defined by an act that aims to influence the decisions within social, economic and political systems and institutions. And if done right, it's a life's work. You can learn from other organizations in your area which are centered around issues you feel strongly about. Research various groups and then partner with people in your community who are working on similar things so you can learn from them.

When your child tells you about an issue at school, whether it is about your child or another, it is important for you to discern all the facts and discuss the situation with your child. You should always contact the teacher or appropriate person at school closest to the situation to share what you have learned, so that person can investigate the matter.

Think about people who have made a difference in our world. Malala Yousafzai was shot in the head at just 15 years old by a Taliban gunman. She remained in critical condition at a hospital, but her condition eventually improved. The attempt on her life launched an outpouring of support. Following her recovery, Malala became a prominent advocate for the right to education, and in 2014 she was awarded the Nobel Peace Prize. Both you and your child can make a difference in this world. Build connections to others and always remember you have access to your state legislature and local government.

Whatever issue you are called to confront, make it a point to understand the problem in its historical context. Your advocacy matters because children can't vote. As parents we need to remember everybody has something they are interested in and willing to fight for. Unfortunately, children don't have all the same citizen rights as adults so you really need to make sure your child has a fair chance at becoming the productive adult you want them to be.

If you do not feel a matter has been resolved, you may want to contact the appropriate supervisor. It is important to know that when you schedule a meeting with a teacher to discuss a specific issue or concern, you may also include other staff. In many schools, teachers work as grade-level teams or in clusters, so they are aware of student progress across all academic subjects. At the high school level, you may want to include the school counselor or an administrator. Ultimately you are responsible for tracking the academic progress of your child.

Always ask specific questions that will address your concerns. Inquire about your child's strengths and weaknesses and how your child is doing in class. Academic success depends on the parent and the teacher working together. The teacher may have insight into the situation that will help your child succeed.

During the meeting each person should express opinions without interruptions. Parents should ask questions if clarification is needed, then ask the teacher for documentation such as test scores or work samples. Remember, it is always best to take a positive approach. Everyone can work in a positive manner and in the best interests of the child.

Get to the root cause of the problem by stating your concerns in a way that focuses on the problem and not the person. For example, when my daughter Christine failed a mathematics test, I was surprised because I was not aware she was doing that poorly. As a parent you can keep abreast of your child's grades by regularly logging on to the parent portal. Teachers are encouraged to maintain relevant current information about each student to share with the parent. If you do not have internet access you should periodically contact your child's teacher or teachers to ensure you are up to date.

After meeting with the teacher, if you are not satisfied you might want to meet with the principal. Again, it is important to conduct the meeting with positive and open dialogue. Your concerns should focus on the issue, not personalities. The school principal will review your concerns with the teacher and seek a resolution.

Sometimes a cause for concern involves hearing about an employee's behavior that you become aware of when your child or another parent brought it to your attention. When you become aware of such a concern you should immediately contact the principal. Do not assume that someone else has reported it. Also, do not assume the allegations are true. Simply tell the principal what you have heard and ask him or her to investigate it immediately. Please note the principal is interested in your information and will fully investigate the matter but cannot discuss personnel matters with you.

Participation in extracurricular activities such as band, cheerleading and athletics is a great way for your child to develop confidence and learn teamwork. Outside the classroom it is important that relationships between coaches and students are conducted in a professional and respectful manner. Athletic coaches are required to have a pre-season parent-athlete information meeting. During this meeting the coach will review all rules and regulations as well as coaching philosophy, goals and objectives. The coach will also communicate his or her expectations of players and review team rules at some point.

You may feel your child is not getting enough playing time. If you have concerns you should schedule a meeting with the coach. It is not appropriate to address concerns before, during or after a game.

Your child's coach will be happy to talk with you when you approach them in a calm manner and show that you care about your child's involvement on the team. The conversation should focus on your child's role and how he or she can improve, rather than on playing time. All comments should be made in a non-judgmental way. Explain how the situation affects you and your child. Remember your child is one of many students on the team, and though you care deeply about your child, the coach must focus on what is best for the entire team.

The coach's opinion of your child's ability may be different from your own. If you are still not satisfied, you should schedule a meeting with the athletic director or the school principal to discuss it further. Above all, maintaining a positive relationship between student, parent and school is extremely important to your child's success.

A Way Forward

Let your child stand on your shoulders and they will see a way forward. For me and my siblings, we stood on the shoulders of parents who supported and love us. We did chores that promoted academic excellence. With your advocacy, love and support, your children will be able to enjoy incremental steps forward.

When children are older, they have seen us advocating for them as a role model. They may later need to practice self-advocacy and understand the impact it can have on their life. When most people think of self-advocacy, they think it's just a selfish way to get something done, however it can be as simple as sending an email to someone in charge.

Because we live in a world that is constantly changing, it can give us the impression that we don't really have a say in what goes on. Whenever your older child starts to feel out of control or thinks they have no say in what happens to them, it's time to self-advocate. They will need to be confident and speak up. You as a parent have given them encouragement, support and love. You have empowered them to go to school. Now you need to remind them to ask for help when needed and to advocate for themselves.

Here are some steps you can share with your children:

1) Believe in yourself and have confidence you are worth it. You are smart, and you can do great things. Sometimes there are certain things that are more challenging. Those are usually the things that just need practice. Don't be afraid to ask for help.

2) Determine a statement that describes what you need help with. Some sentence starters include: "Would it be okay if I talk to you?" "I would like to ask you some questions about this assignment," and "I'm having trouble understanding this. May I stay after class to speak with you?"

3) Figure out who is the best person to talk to. Who do you feel most comfortable with? It might be a teacher, counselor or a principal or coach. It might even be a classmate. Set up a meeting with that person. Don't be nervous. They are there to help you.

4) It might sound silly, but practice what you want to talk about. Stand in front of a mirror or a family member.

Practicing it will make you more comfortable when you talk with that person.

5) Sometimes we get nervous and forget what was discussed. Bring a notepad with you and write down any suggestions that person might give you. Refer back to these notes when you're done.

Encourage your children to start thinking about a subject they could improve in. What assignments do they need help with? What steps can you suggest they do?

When older children learn to self-advocate you are teaching them to take charge of their life and their future success. With some practice and help from you, your children can achieve any goals they set!

Optimize Your 15 Minutes a Day
so that you and your child can
Win the Day... Everyday!

Visit 15MinutesADayBook.com/Win

---

7 | SUPERVISING THE ACADEMIC SUCCESS OF YOUR CHILD

Your child's academic success has to do with your ability to create time for schoolwork, reading for pleasure and other learning activities together.

Knowing how much help to give with schoolwork is the most essential component. Younger children require more hand-holding because they have not yet developed an internal structure for homework. They need to learn to stay focused. They will need the external support only you can provide them.

For older children, you will need to watch them solve the first few problems to ensure they understand the assigned material, but then step out. Sometimes sitting with your children while they do homework is not effective if it sends the message that they are not capable of doing the work themselves.

Always remember that assignment is for the child—not for you to show you can do the homework. You should not need to touch the paper, nor correct every single problem. Only be sure the work is completed.

You will need to know when to provide support, but equally important is knowing when not to intervene. If you see your child struggling, work together until the child can demonstrate an understanding of the content. Then let them work on their own. When it comes to schoolwork, independence is one of the significant boundaries you can give your children for academic excellence.

Your family probably has a schedule for watching television and recreation. Reading is a timeless and exciting way for your child to explore the world. When it comes to technology and screen time, however, technology should be limited. Television, tablets, and cell phones are few of the technologies available for children use, but health experts say the amount of time children spend using those devices should be limited. The American Academy of Pediatrics recommends that children two years of age or younger should have no screen time, and for ages 2–5 years, a maximum of one hour high-quality programming (like Sesame Street) per day under parental supervision.

You should encourage device-free playtime to help children develop social skills, regardless of age. It's important to set limits. Parental guidance is important, and you are the parent, so you determine the restrictions. You can also choose to set technology-free zones at certain times or places like the dinner table or right before bedtime.

It is important for you to create time to join your children in recreation activities. The benefits promote both joy and academic excellence. Also, children need plenty of daily exercise. A moderate to vigorous amount of activity will improve bone health, weigh status, reduce depression, and increase cognitive functioning. So, help to get the wiggles out and decrease that pent-up energy!

Some ideas to keep children healthy and active:

Let's start with outdoor ideas, games and activities. Parents can make plans for Red light/green light, Red Rover, and Freeze-tag. Children like group games and it's a great way for them to get some exercise. However, don't let the kids have all the fun; jump in there and participate with them!

Playing sports is another great idea. Soccer, basketball, football, tennis and frisbee are all favorites. A hike or nature walk is one of my family's favorites. Children love to explore the outdoors, finding new trails and seeing new things. Be prepared timewise with hikes, because it might take a little longer than the time you budgeted. You will likely have to stop and inspect a lot of things along the way!

Bikes, scooters, skateboards, and rollerblades are also great ways to get children outside and active. When I think back on my childhood, my bike was my freedom. I used to ride to friends' houses and to get away. But hoverboards and motorized scooters require different precautions! It is preferable for children to use their own muscle power to get from place to place. Coach children to wear a properly fitted protective helmet whenever they ride to avoid injury.

Sidewalk chalk is a cheap and easy way to promote art and creativity, but there are different ways to make it more active. Draw a hopscotch path, targets, bases or obstacles that children can run to and from. This is a great way to get children up and active, having fun outside.

Get children up and active, having fun outside.

Next, let's go inside. Simon Says will keep your kids active and engaged. Big motions like jumping jacks, reaching overhead, twisting, and running in place are all keep children entertained, and make exercise like a game. Charades is another great indoor game to play with children... just check your ego at the door because this game will make you look silly! Limbo is another great indoor activity. Everyone can use different ways to go under the bar. See who can go lowest, or get the most creative.

Hide-and-seek is a time-honored favorite. Twister can be played with or without the game board. Just draw different colored dots, or cut them out of construction paper, and designate which hands or feet should go on which color.

Scavenger hunt can be a great activity, especially if there are stairs in your house. Parents can hide one clue upstairs, then one clue downstairs. Children will race up and down without even realizing how much they are playing. All this hide-and-seek, scavenger hunt, and Twister will promote balance, strength and coordination in children.

Finally, there are a lot of fun and interactive video games for Nintendo Switch, Wii, Xbox and PlayStation. All have different games that will follow your movements and cast them onto the screen. This is a great way kids can still get in their video games. They think they are playing online, but it is more exercise and activity for them. Of course, I recommend parents should participate!

Reading for pleasure should always be an option, but only a handful of families actually put this into practice. Recently, we've seen YouTube and podcasts used as a substitute for reading. These two technologies have their advantages and disadvantages. A book is like a portrait as opposed to a photograph. The photo is a static image, but a portrait has layer upon layer, still creating an image, but with more depth. A book enables you to think and then rethink as you go deeper.

But that doesn't mean you can't go deep in podcasts and audio books. Audio books are just as valuable. We can't read while we are driving, doing dishes, or exercising. However, with audio, you have all the time opened up that used to be only for music.

It's true that our children have a fragmented attention span. You should encourage children to read, which promotes a more disciplined mind. I believe the downfall of humanity is the negligence of teaching the importance of discipline. Never mind responsibility, accountability or sacrifice.

Reading is my favorite activity. Everything about the process is enjoyable to me—including the excitement of buying a new book and looking forward to sitting down and getting lost in its story. Books held develop a child's reading comprehension, analytical abilities and vocabulary. It is less passive than listening to a podcast, audio book, or video lecture. Not to devalue discussions, films, or other more passive media, which are valuable, But I think reading simply cannot be replaced if you're looking for a means to improve your child's mind.

Getting children ready for school in the mornings

Many parents face the daily challenge of getting their children ready for school. Here are some easy steps you can take to prevent those stressful mornings.

1. **Establish a bedtime routine.** When there is a set time for children go to bed they will wake up on time more easily. This will also help parents ensure children are getting enough sleep. School-age children need around ten to eleven hours of sleep per night.

2. **Before the week begins, set out a week's worth of school uniforms or school clothes.** Use the school calendar to guide you, so you know which day includes gym class or sports, then place any other necessary uniforms or equipment on the appropriate shelf. This will save time in the morning and avoid hassles.

3. **Have a food plan.** Know in advance exactly what you're going to make for breakfast and pack for school lunch. Creating a breakfast and lunch menu works well.

4. **Remove all distractions**. Make sure the television is off during bedtime and that children do not have toys with them at breakfast.

5. **Have your child ready their school bag the night before**. Locate their shoes and leave them with the bag by the front door since these two items always go missing in the morning. It will be one less thing to worry about, plus it's a great way to teach children to be responsible and organized.

Independence and responsibility

Parental supervision of academic success is necessary to promote children to do their best and take responsibility. But a big worry for most parents is how we can make our children more independent and responsible. The answer to this question will require you to let your child struggle with a school project sometimes. Allow them to do their own activities and work. Assign chores like cleaning up their own messy room and dirty dishes. Children are adorable, but you cannot tolerate living in a filthy place.

When you do everything for your child, you limit their potential for future independence. If the child is watching television and asks for a glass of water, and you give it to them, you have taken on responsibility that should belong to the child. If the child drops milk on the floor and you ask the maid to clean it, you have not taught your child to take ownership for one's own accidents and mistakes.

It is not love to do things for children just because you don't want them to get their hands dirty. I know you want your children to enjoy the luxuries that you never got in life. But if you want a responsible child, then let them do their own work, even if it means they lose a few points, their room is dirty, or they hate you for five minutes.

Second, don't overprotect your child. Your first instinct will always be to keep your child safe, but if you want an independent and responsible child you will need to develop tolerance for them crying, being scared, or hurt. These negative emotions are the breeding ground for some of life's most important lessons. For example, another child accidentally hit your child at school. This is not a reason for a parent to rush to school and threaten, "If you ever lay a hand on my child again, I will beat the crap out of you." If your child fails a school test, shouting at the teacher will not be helpful. If your child is too afraid to talk to the neighbor to retrieve something simple thing like a ball, positively do not say, "Don't worry. I will go get it for you."

You need to understand that children need to learn how to cope with new situations, including stressful ones. You can step in the door with your wisdom, as if the child were in the boxing ring with you standing on the side coaching. Do not step in the ring to take over the fight. Let your child learn from the experience. You may have to let them get bruised, but make sure they come back to you afterward so you can discuss what happened.

The goal of talking is so that children can develop strategies that will work better next time. It also helps so they don't make wrong conclusions about what they experienced and inadvertently get traumatized by it. The goal of talking is to give them a story and motivation, so they can get back up and try again. This time with a little more information than before!

Let them experience obstacles. Let them be uncomfortable. You should build a connection good enough that your child will feel comfortable talking to you about such obstacles... and when they do talk, give them the best wisdom you have.

Third, don't make all the decisions for your child. If you want children to be responsible, give them choices and more decision-making authority. For example: "Which shirt would you like to wear today?" "Which class subject's homework will you do first?"

When instead you preach, "Don't go outside, it's dangerous," or "Don't talk to the neighborhood children, you'll learn the wrong things," what it really conveys is that you as a parent have made a lot of mistakes in life. There will be a moment when children will say, "I don't care if this is a mistake." In those moments it's better to let children figure it out on their own instead of forcing them to "shut up and obey."

However, you should still be concerned if the choice can have a dangerous outcome. Will there be short-term or long-term consequences? If there's nothing catastrophic, let them have their way. Let them experience the consequences, but don't say, "I told you so," or "You never listen to me." That's not helpful. When children make a mistake that's your invitation to start a discussion with them. Most probably the child has already learned the lesson, but if have not, you can offer the lesson in your discussion.

When children make a bad choice, the firsthand experience will make them stronger in the future. Next time they can hopefully handle something bigger. When this process is repeated over the years, your child will be able to step outside the house confidently, and you can feel confident as well that he or she can handle any challenges.

> *When children make poor choices, the firsthand experience will make them stronger in the future.*

The threshold is that children can avoid disastrous mistakes in adulthood by having a few early experiences and talking them over with parents. This approach is like a training ground. Parents can create low-risk simulations so children can practice and avoid crash landings in the real world.

If you want an independent and responsible child, don't take away the opportunities for your child to engage, explore, explain, extend and evaluate while you are supervising.

SCREEN TIME

Managing your child's use of television, video games, and cell phone apps means you should know what your child sees. Use the subject as a chance to talk about values. Excess screen time is a problem for children academic success. Nowadays, children's screen time ranges from 4–10 hours a day. Hence, parents are expressing dissatisfaction about their children's study habits.

These children sometimes do not eat, do not get to sleep on time, do not interact with family members, the only friends they have are online, and they do not go out to play because they seemingly enjoy just lying in bed all day lost in their virtual world. In a nutshell, this screen time has consumed our children.

Here are some tips for what *not* to do, because it will make things worse:

Do NOT Make a Plea. You may think if you are nice and ask calmly, "Please don't use the phone so much. It's not good for you," that they will listen and comply. Requesting rarely works for this issue.

Do NOT Rely on the Child to Stop. You may think your child has the self-control to set the phone down. "I want my child to make the responsible decision." This is not a good idea because screen time is so enjoyable to the brain that children won't be able to stop by themselves.

Do NOT nag or shout. This is the negative version of requesting. If might be tempted to increase the intensity of plea. "Please leave the phone. What are you doing all day? You've wasted so many hours. When will you study?" Then you are likely to get more upset and say those same things in anger, shouting at your child, which will only serve to drive you further apart.

What WILL Work:

Prevention. Establish your authority inside the house before your child reaches ten years of age, when it is much easier for you to say no to something. Parents often allow phones, iPads and laptops to keep children "busy" so they won't create a mess, or fight with siblings. However, releasing the device gets harder as children grow up and their addiction becomes deeper. Be strict with this. Do not let the child challenge your authority when they are younger, because unforeseen trouble is coming.

Limit screen time. Children under 10 should be limited to 1–2 hours per day. As children get older, 2–3 hours is a good limit, not counting screen time required for schoolwork. Clearly communicate with your child the specific number of hours which are allowed. For example, "You have a one-hour limit of screen time after homework and house chores are done." Make it a rule and do not let them let them break it.

Screen policing. You will need to constantly check on children during screen time, much like a customs officer. If you have been traveling and try to cross the border with illegal items, the customs officer will seize your stuff—no negotiation, no prosecution. You must maintain the law and order in your house, which involves making sure the well thought out rules are being followed. When a rule is broken, you must carry out the consequence without shouting or anger. This teaches the child that screen time rules are truly important to you, and that they must abide by these rules or suffer the consequences.

Be reasonable and consistent. Let your child understand the reasons behind your decision to limit screen time—to prevent addiction, for healthy eyes, to avoid a sedentary lifestyle, to engage with real people. If children disagree, you must keep telling them because consistency matters. It is important for you to be aware that there will be some resistance, possibly even tantrums, in the process of implementing clear rules, then policing them. Do not accept defeat.

Have a substitute for screen time. When you take something away from the child, give them something in return. Consider toys, comics books, or board games. These can be social or educational. Perhaps enroll the child in music or dance classes, exercise with them, sign them up for sports, and talk to them for at least an hour every day. Find ways that children can hang out with their friends. Make sure they get enough sleep. Again, stick to these new and better activities and communicate with children during the transition.

To summarize, you must set a clear limit for screen time. You must enforce that rule with full authority to create the least harm, and you must support this rule with consistent and rational communication.

Parental knowledge of school achievement and personal growth

You should develop good communication with you children, their teachers, and other stakeholders at the school. You need to check your child's progress online daily and review report cards, attend parent-teacher conferences and ask relevant questions from the children about their activities. For example, "What's something that made you happy today in school?" During conferences, ask, "Can you share an example of leadership or thoughtfulness you have observed in my child?"

You must be involved in your children's education if you want them to be successful and happy. There are three phases of happiness: pleasure, engagement and meaning. So, to help children find their "why"—their purpose—follow these steps.

Discover what inspires your child. Knowing their inspiration is like fuel for the rocket. Without it, that rocket cannot take off and soar. When children are inspired, they will not stop thinking and talking about it. Therefore, observe what makes their eyes big, what they talk about all the time, and what do they not want to stop doing.

Identify your child's talents. Talent is like the guidance system for the rocket. It will help your child navigate through space and reach the destination. Every child has their own innate talents. Observe what they do consistently and especially what they enjoy.

Create time to be together. Playing cards and other games engages you and your child and elicits their natural talents. Then you can have a discussion about them.

Develop the skills. Skills are like the structure of the rocket. It's how you add value for your child. There two types of skills: hard skills and soft skills. The hard skills are those learned abilities, acquired through formal education and training, like computer programming, writing, and mathematics. Soft skills include communication, leadership, teamwork, time management, and flexibility. Soft skills change with the environment. Discover what skills your child needs. For example, if your child earned all As in science and mathematics, but failed social studies, focus on the math and science. This is where the child's inspiration and talents are. Then use a remedial system for the social studies.

When you observe what inspires your child, identify the talents, then support that inspiration, you will go a long way toward helping your child develop and improve the already innate skills.

Optimize Your 15 Minutes a Day
so that you and your child can
Win the Day... Everyday!

Visit 15MinutesADayBook.com/Win

---

8 | Encouraging Academic Performance

Lending your encouragement is an important skill, but it must come from the heart. If your child comes home with a good grade on a paper, instead of saying, "Wow, great job. I am so proud of you," (which does work) consider instead saying, "Wow, way to go. I bet you're proud of yourself. How do you feel?"

Encouragement leads people to think, figure things out, and feel good about their accomplishment. Praise doesn't necessarily do that. Praise only works when the child feels good about the parent or source of the praise.

Parental encouragement is like the work of a potter, and there's an intimate relationship to the work. This is true of any creator with his or her art, a poem, music, even a garden. When you see that potter's wheel, the potter's hands and where the clay object begins, the object and the hands are covered in that same filmy silt. So, the created object is fine and delicate, yet ultimately durable. Parents should build such intimate relationships with their children.

Children are easily influenced when young. Well-trained children can be graceful, elegant and straightforward... and also resilient. Use your authority to support, encourage, motivate behavior so your child becomes a good citizen of society.

This is an ongoing process, rather than once and done. Sometimes the clay on a potter's wheel turns out badly. You can gently shape and reshape your child's behavior until formed into something new. This is what great parents do. They do not give up but keep working hard at being a good role model for their children. Potters don't just put a piece of clay on the wheel without guiding it into a desired shape. Likewise, you should encourage children but not overwhelm them. If a potter were to handle an object, it would be with a gentle hand, turning something beloved into something artistic and then into something durable.

> *Parental encouragement is like the work of a potter— intimately involved.*

Start early to develop a positive relationship with your teenage children. This is very important, because it will promote your ability to influence your teen, and prompt them to come to you for guidance and support. However, this is especially challenging for many reasons.

Teens are becoming independent and spending more time away from home. This is frequently a time of new experiences and self-discovery. But spending quality time with your teen will help you both to grow closer together, and improve trust, honesty, fairness and open communication.

To enhance the relationship you have with your teen, spend time with them and just have fun. Sometimes it might mean a trip to a coffee shop that you both enjoy. Showing affection to your teen is important. A pat on their back can make a big difference, so they will feel comfortable coming to you.

Teens are developing critical thinking and negotiating skills. When there is a problem or issue, get their perspective before responding. For example, if the teacher gave your teen a failing grade, encourage your child to think about their work and discuss how it can be improved. Use problem-solving together. This demonstrates respect and fairness which will enhance the teen-parent relationship.

Work together to assist teens to resolve their own problem. This is all part of a healthy relationship and preparation for successful adulthood. Teens need their parent's faith in them as well as positive encouragement. Try to use positive feedback at least eighty percent of the time. For example, thank your teen for putting dishes away or for starting dinner.

You will need to learn more about teen culture, including their music and the television shows they watch. Never give up. And forgive easily. It's never too late to strengthen your relationship with your teen. Keep your sense of humor, because these challenging but fun years last only a short time, while your relationship with the child is lifelong.

Find ways to connect with other parents of teens through your faith group, school sporting events or work. Compare notes and share ideas in order to support and learn from one another.

Another way to encourage academic success is to engage in reading. Consider gifting an e-reading device to your teen. They often find the tech more fun. The Kindle, Nook, or Kobo-style devices are lightweight, extremely portable and hold thousands of books. So, whether your child is an avid or reluctant reader, it will keep them engaged.

I strongly encourage you to pack your own books and some for the children when it is family trip time. Make sure to select titles that reflect your children's interests. If your child is a reluctant reader, look for books with easier language to avoid frustration. When you are reading with your child, stop occasionally and ask a few questions to make sure they get what's going on and if they don't know, look it up instantly.

Another idea is to take turns reading with your child. Have them read the first chapter to you, then you read the second chapter. This helps ensure that children stay engaged. Book clubs can also be a great way to encourage children to read. Not only do children look forward to seeing their friends, but as we all know, they love to share their opinions. So, let children talk about what they liked about the book, and even the things they didn't like so much.

Taking trips to the library can be so much fun. Also, e-readers can be used to browse and borrow titles for free from the public library. When the book "expires" it automatically returns to the library's online collection, which saves you trips and dreaded late fees. Remember your child's interests and create a passionate reader for life.

Good habits

Be it a school assignment, church project, or community project, make sure to model good behaviors for your children. The study area of your home should be separate and away from activities of the rest of the household. Make sure children have supplies, including all the resources they need, and are prepared to set aside time. Nowadays, lives are very complicated, and families are running in all directions. Make sure to set a timer for homework so they have plenty of time to start and finish their work.

Make sure children have all the supplies they need, including resources and time.

The next thing that will promote academic excellence is to ensure that children become more responsible. As mentioned earlier, you can give children choices like, "Do you want the red apple or the green apple?" This allows opportunity for low-risk failure. Sometimes good wisdom only develops from bad experiences. Give children opportunities to make decisions right from the beginning. That way the decisions they make when they are out of your sight—when they are 16 and older—are going to be much better.

A next step is problem-solving. Rather than blame or punish children, instead think in terms of problem solving. When a child has done something wrong say, "Well, we have a problem here." The child is not the problem, but rather the child has created a problem, so both parent and child will look for a solution together. For example, if one of your children broke their sibling's toy, ask what can be done to problem-solve. Making reparations is how children learn. Even when we mean well, we are still human and sometimes make mistakes. We can always make things better. Problem-solving empowers our children instead of making them feel like bad people.

Next, set limits in an empathetic way. Teaching children to be responsible and emotionally intelligent people will demand that you interact on a scale between permissive and authoritarian. If you demand too much, children may feel you are very strict and inflexible. They will be less likely to bring tough issues to you later. On the opposite side, you do not want your children to run around a restaurant and annoy everybody else like they are spoiled rotten. The sweet spot is a place that takes individual situations into consideration and responds in a way that feels rational and merited.

> *Teaching responsibility requires that you interact on a scale somewhere between permissive and authoritarian.*

The solution is to stay supportive and encouraging. You might say, "I see it's not really appropriate to have brought you to this restaurant." In the case of a broken toy say, "You can be upset with your sibling, but do not destroy someone else's property. We need to do something about this problem you've created." That's the sweet spot in parenting with empathetic limits.

WORD OF ENCOURAGEMENT

The goal of every parent is to raise successful children. Academic excellence need encouragement, with words like "I believe in you." Be careful what words you speak. Your words really do make an impact. If children are told they are believed in, and that they can reach for their dreams, then they will thrive. Make sure your child hears these positive words in your family.

Have declarations you say every night to your child. "You are brave and you are powerful. You are a miracle and you are smart. You are good at listening. You speak nicely with kind words. You are a good friend and sibling. You can sleep through the night. You are loved." The words and actions you affirm are the behaviors and beliefs that will follow your child for a lifetime.

Optimize Your 15 Minutes a Day
so that you and your child can
Win the Day... Everyday!

Visit 15MinutesADayBook.com/Win

---

9 | Demographics and Parental Involvement

To keep our nation and future generations in constructive and effective hands, former President Obama placed great emphasis on the increase of parental involvement in children's education. He made many presentations on how parental involvement helps students progress on to higher levels of education. This simply includes activities such as meeting with the child's teacher routinely, sitting by the children's side while they are doing homework, and making sure they have nutritious meals throughout the week.

When parents get involved, there are positive relationships between family demographics such as parents' age, annual income, educational level and students' academic excellence outcomes. Parental involvement yields positive expectations and reflects the strongest association with educational achievement. In addition, parents who have plans for their children to attend universities or colleges are associated with higher academic achievement across ethnic groups. This is consistent and reflects the importance of setting high expectations for your children.

> *Parents who plan for their children to attend college are more likely to have students with higher academic success.*

Parental involvement continues to be difficult because of responsibilities of work, school, and family that affect some families differently. In most cases mothers appear to be more affected by these issues than fathers. This is true of both single and married mothers. Another barrier to the problem of lack of parental involvement happens in city schools and urban areas.

MATHEMATICS ACHIEVEMENT STUDY

Children tend to do better when schools, families, and community groups work together to support learning. Also, these same children will tend to stay in school longer, enjoy school more and finish their education.

Here are the benefits of parental involvement in children education:

- Students get higher grades, test scores, and graduation rates increase
- Attendance soars
- Greater enrollment in post-secondary education
- Teachers and administrators have higher morale

- Increased teacher effectiveness and greater job satisfaction

Parent's communication with teachers also improves immensely. Children also have increased education skills and their attitude toward school and school personnel improve. Children of diverse cultural backgrounds have a tendency to perform better when parents and professionals work together, bridging cultural gaps between home and school. In implementing such practices, backgrounds such as parents' education, family's size, and marital status are unimportant.

Research has proven that schools which engage families from diverse backgrounds build trust, and recognize, respect and address family needs. Power responsibilities are thus shared. Low-income families are offered programs through the community, church or home visits which are more successful than programs requiring parents to come to the school. This aids parents to not only be involved in early years of a child's education but continued involvement at all ages and grade levels. In the process, children in middle school and high school will make better transitions, keep up the quality of their work and develop real life plans.

Benefits regarding school quality include:

- Organizations have higher student achievement
- Teacher morale is higher
- Parents rate teachers on a higher scale
- School accountability produces positive changes in policy/practices
- Leadership/staffing improves
- Funding for more assistance increases
- Support from families and communities

- Great test results statewide

Students are more likely to exhibit positive attitudes and behavior when parents get involved in their education. Students are self-confident and tend to believe in the importance of school. If they exhibit bad or negative behaviors such as substance abuse and violence, these too tend to decrease.

Researchers believe the biggest message for families is "School is what you make it." Some parents believe they do not have a lot of time, but as little as fifteen minutes of uninterrupted time spent with children each day will increase mastery, academic skills, raise self-esteem and go a long way toward a successful academic career.

When parents are involved, students earn higher grades and test scores. They earn credit and are promoted. As previous research stated, they attend school regularly and graduate and go on to pursue post-secondary education. Southwest Educational Development Laboratory also stated students possess better social skills, improved behavior and are well-adjusted to school.

As little as 15 minutes each day with your child will go a long way!

Southwest Educational Development Laboratory indicates programs that works best are the ones that engage families in supporting their children's learning at home, linking them to higher student achievement. Project Early Access to Success in Education, a literacy program in Minnesota, stated home and school activities on literacy for kindergartners and their families generated significant positive gains. Project Early Access to Success in Education, employed parent educators who coached parents to help their children develop literacy skills. These literacy-related activities had outcomes of greater scores by the end of the program.

When parents are involved, teachers can ensure they are trained in using the course materials to help their children at home. This involvement makes stronger reading and mathematics gains than with less involved parents. What was truly beneficial as revealed by this program was that income played no part. Lower-income families and higher-income families alike were well represented. Parental involvement and learning at home had the greatest effect on children's test scores. Parents also encouraged their children to take rigorous courses aiming for college.

Part of this program, which encourages participation by parents or family members from elementary through high school is a mathematics activity packet. The student must complete a worksheet on fractions. This was designed so that the student had to explain figures in terms of fractions using the family member assisting him. These packets are then signed by the parent and sent back to the school/teacher.

For high school students, the interaction is a bit more intense. Students are required to conduct interviews of their parents regarding topics like social studies. For example, the student asks, "Have things improved or worsened regarding poverty, health care, education, crime, race relation, and individual freedom?" The student, in turn, must write down these views on a separate piece of paper. The parent must write whether or not the work done assisted them with understanding their child's assignment/work in school.

Parental involvement extends to other areas outside of homework. Parents attend workshops, teaching them the importance of getting their children to school, allowing home visits and using contracts of commitment to make sure their children have good attendance. This ensures regular communication with parents and teachers, help students adjust better in school and what is expected of them in class, their achievement soars. Parent-Teacher Association (PTA) meetings are good, but tools used for parents to enhance learning for their children are better.

Community-based Organizations (CBOs) are stakeholders that play an important role in helping schools engage parents. Although parental involvement is a plus, it does not solve all problems, parents will still need to check homework, talk to their children about school, attend events, and volunteer. Teachers need to take time working with students constructively rather than clinically. A child needs to feel connected to school and have a feeling of belonging there and at home.

DEVELOPING TEACHER/PARENT LEADERSHIP

When we focused on parents' perceptions of and expectation for teaching and learning of mathematics, many parents were anxious about not being able to help their children with their homework. This was because they had no understanding of the course content. Parental involvement benefit is designed to help parents and teachers learn the different styles for learning, to facilitate and coach children. All parents are welcomed with their children from K–12.

Here, parents eventually become more informed with the teacher's help, thus becoming more confident in subject matter. Parents can explore mathematics topics as needed. This helps parents become more proficient, thus able with homework more confidently.

Some parents used creative ways for informal learning opportunities at home. Such things as separation of Christmas lights, then bulbs evenly to fit in a certain number of bags, playing card games to teach numbers, and cooking and teaching measurements make great real-world learning tools. Using computer software, flash cards and board games, they also taught about money and about giving and receiving change.

Parental involvement in children's education had a high success rate. This included attendance at meetings, whether with teachers, in-school events and serving or volunteering on committees. There were significant positive effects with parental involvement in elementary and secondary school levels, but the largest was observed at the elementary level.

What Does Parental Involvement Entail?

You can monitor your children's school and classroom activities and coordinate efforts with teachers, encouraging acceptable classroom behavior and overseeing homework. Teachers are more positive and feel adequate about their job performance when there is interaction with parents. This includes involvement with fathers as well as mothers, whether the father lives in the same home.

Hispanic and black parents were less involved in school meeting, activities, events, and volunteering compared to parents of white students, although at not too significant of a margin.

There are many obstacles that play a role in some parents' ability to be an active participant when it comes to involvement in their children's education. Some of these obstacles include language barriers, transportation, chronic health conditions, and work/employment conflicts. Some schools have tried to counteract these barriers by implementing back-to-school nights and school-based cultural events. They have also tried making school hubs of social services for the neighborhood.

Stakeholders engage more in the educational process when researchers are following and implementing the following steps:

- Survey educators and familiar to determine needs, interests, and ideas about collaborating.

- Develop and pass family-friendly policies and laws. This includes such things as caregivers and leaves of absence for parents to become active participants in school activities and meetings.

- Teach school employees about family and community engagement.

- Train parents and community stakeholders on effective communications and partnering skills.

- Offer better information about school and school policies and procedures.

- Promote effective communication tools which address a variety of family structures, give information in a timely manner, and offer translation for such materials.

- Hire/train school personnel and liaisons regarding the communities' history, language, and cultural background to contact parents and coordinate activities.

- Reach out to higher education institutions to allow teachers and administrators to have programs to prepare them for implementing parent/family/community involvement.

- Develop outreach programs so that families, businesses, and communities may be presented with involvement opportunities, policies, and information strategies.

- Be diligent in evaluating the progression and effectiveness of family involvement programs/activities.

It is strongly evident that all parties involved must come together as one unit to have positive results in children's education. These parties include parents, teachers, and other education personnel, including districts.

When there is avid communication, results tend to become positive and rewarding for everyone involved. It is important that children know there is positive communication with their parents and teachers/facilitators. They can seek help both at school and home without being pulled in directions that are not conducive to productive results in school, on tests and with homework.

PARENTAL INVOLVEMENT AND SECONDARY SCHOOL STUDENTS

There is growing concern about the destiny of our adolescents. A myriad of reports has emerged in the last few years pointing to problems associated with this developmental period—an increasing incidence of school failure, growing dropout rates, especially in the large urban school districts, increasing involvement of youth in delinquent and very dangerous activities, increasing violence among youth, and increasing incidents of poor adjustment. Also, African-American adolescents are already in danger and these adolescents are at risk for major problems.

Adolescence is a time when students blossom into fascinating and healthy young adults, if they are provided with supportive and developmentally appropriate social contexts to explore themselves and the world around them. Parents have an important impact in their children's academic outcome, as well in their socio-economic development. It is only recently, however, that we have begun to look at the impact schools might play in facilitating and coaching parents' positive role in children's academic outcome. The important of this role is the relationship that develops between parents and schools, and communities and schools. It is important for schools to make their school climate conducive to welcome parents when they visit for any reason, because this visit helps the school increase student academic achievement.

> *It is important for schools to create a conducive climate to welcome parental visits.*

There is evidence that even though many suggestions have been made regarding strategies to motivate parents to participate in school activities, some parents choose to withdraw from such activities. Factors influencing parent participation include the child's gender and age. Parental involvement drops off rather dramatically as children move into middle and high school. Why? It is likely that some of this decrease reflects the stereotypic belief that parents should begin to disengage from their adolescents as they move into secondary schools.

Parents may feel that adolescents desire independence, and thus feel that their involvement is less important. They may also feel the children do not want them to come to school, as evidenced by a common adolescent plea not to have their parents chaperone school activities. Although there may be an element of truth in this belief, it is too extreme. Adolescents may indeed want greater autonomy, but they still need to know that their parents support their endeavors. They need a safe haven in which to explore their independence, a safe haven in which both parents and schools are actively involved. It is important that schools do what they can to strengthen the role available to parents during these years.

The decrease in parental involvement, as children move into secondary schools, may also result from a decrease in parents' feelings of efficacy. It may be that parents feel less able to help children with schoolwork as the content becomes more advanced and technical. No longer are children working on basic reading and spelling skills or drilling mathematics facts. Parents may not know the material being taught in more advanced and specialized courses. Parents may also feel that the methods used in teaching various subjects (for example mathematics) are very different from those used when they were in school. Therefore, they may worry that they will mislead or confuse their children if they try to help.

Finally, research has shown that parents believe they have more influence over their children in general, as well as in terms of specific behaviors, when the children are in the elementary grades than they will have when their children reach adolescence. It is more important than ever that parents maintain connection throughout their children's school years to support them in this quest for academic excellence.

Optimize Your 15 Minutes a Day
so that you and your child can
Win the Day… Everyday!

Visit 15MinutesADayBook.com/Win

---

10 | Conclusion

How can you learn to expect more for your children and help them move forward in their own personal achievements? Whether it be academics, the arts or sports, look for what inspires your child already and build on their natural talents and skills. As U.S. immigrants from Nigeria, West Africa, it was our family's dream for our three beautiful children to be successful. Therefore, from a very early age we told our children they should strive for excellence, and that's exactly what they did.

When I first started working with middle school students, I too pushed them to strive for excellence. I found that many of my students rose to the challenge. I always tell them it is not okay to just pass through life doing only enough to get by when they have the talent and skills. I want every parent to continue pushing children to work hard for excellence. This becomes a habit just like anything else. The more you do something, the more ingrained it becomes.

Children recognize that teachers, guidance counselors, and parents are their support system. Middle school students want the best cell phones, the most retweets and shares on something they posted, and of course they want the newest clothes. When you encourage kids to engage and do better in the home and with their grades, when they realize their true academic potential, hopefully that spills over to other aspects of their lives.

As an adult and educator, I suggest you motivate and empower your children. Empowering children means talking with them, praising, positively reward them, getting to know their likes and dislikes and their future goals.

Remember to make learning fun and relevant. Excellence is not an exception; it is a prevailing attitude. For me growing up, my parents were the most important people in my life. I wanted nothing more than to be just like my mother. She was dedicated to her family and Catholic faith. I grew up having both parents involved in my education. This was a critical component to my success. Now as a parent, grandparent, and educator, I know how important parent involvement in students' academic life is.

> *As a child, I wanted nothing more than to be just like my mother.*

Every bit of research agrees. Students of any age need their parents involved in their academic lives, especially if they want to be successful. Parents who are involved in their children's education in ways that create and reinforce direct experiences of educational success offer verbal persuasion intended to develop attitudes, behaviors and efforts consistent with school success and create emotional arousal that underscores the personal importance of doing well in school and sense of efficacy for successfully achieving in school-related activities.

As children grow older, parent involvement begins to decrease at home and in the school. Parents begin to believe that their involvement is not as important in later grades. This contributes to the student's desire for independence and parents trying to fulfill that desire. Other reasons include education level and financial income of the parent. Parents with lower educational levels tend to stay away from helping their student with homework and activities because they feel inadequate about course content. Also, parents with lower financial gains are unable to help due to a lack of time because of work schedules and other family priorities.

Research has shown that there is a large disconnect between school and parent communication in these families. Most of these parents did not have a conference with the teacher during the school year, had never talked with a teacher by telephone, and most reported they had never discussed their children's programs or progress. The clear, consistent and obvious fact is, there is a disconnect between parents and schools and it is affecting the academic involvement in children's lives, which in turn affects academic success.

Parents can be more successful at home by knowing what is going on the classroom if they have the teacher's syllabus and can stay up to date on what is coming up in the classroom. Help your children be prepared. Your involvement is crucial to your child's achievement and future success.

You need to get involved as early as possible, starting with preschool. The philosophy for this is that it is easiest to get involved when children are at a young age and you are most comfortable. It allows you to grow with your child through their academic education. You are less likely to become intimidated later on if you have been connected all along.

A good place to take active steps to help your child succeed is in the home's general environment. Create a space that's conducive for growth and good study habits. Invest steadily to make your home nurturing for every single person there, beginning with the father and mother and all the children.

Build an environment for children to blossom, which includes being real and making mistakes. Remember to grant second chances. There will be times to be serious, to be loud, to hug and to be together. The home environment needs to be nurturing, so everyone feels a sense of belonging. Children need to feel like an important part of the family, like they are part of the process... even if they make mistakes. Parents should want children to be able to boast, "I know for sure that my parents love me."

Develop helpful affirmations for your child's self-esteem. They can learn, read out loud, and memorize the affirmations, speaking them even when things are difficult. I encourage my children to repeat affirmations, because the more times we hear positive things about ourselves the more we begin to believe them. For example, "There is no one like you. I am so proud of you. You are a hard worker." These are phrases that make children feel empowered about their capacity.

> *Children need to feel like an important part of the family... even if they make mistakes.*

Design weekly rewards and incentives for responsible behavior. When homework is completed on time and chores are done, designate an amount of time for fun and games together. Make sure it's a reward the child looks forward to, and something they are genuinely interested in. If you have a child who likes to sleep in, tell them if they can finish all their schoolwork by Friday night, they can sleep in longer on Saturday.

Try to create rewards the children look forward to. It doesn't always have to be monetary, but it must be something that motivates your child to meet the goal. It might mean serving their favorite dish or going out to the movies. There are many choices you can offer as incentives to help kids achieve their weekly goals and targets.

Time management will be important, both for you and your child. Remember to limit screen time and cell phone use because sleep routines matter deeply. If a child is not sleeping long enough, they will likely wake up groggy and that will have an impact on their performance at school.

Create regimens that involve taking responsibility. Chores can include packing their bags ahead of each day and setting out their own clothes.

Lines of communication must be kept open in all directions to promote connection and keep conversation tension free. Listen to your child before you offer solutions. Sometimes it's best to allow children to solve their own problems. When the child gets into trouble with a teacher, ask them what they are going to do. Letting children think through what actions they did, and how that behavior created consequences, is excellent for prompting long-term behavior change.

Our society wants people who are disciplined, who can think on their own, who can take initiative. So, listen before you solve the problem and always discuss what your children are learning at school. When discussing with the children remember to bring real life connections to the concepts they're learning at school.

Next develop a schedule for reviewing weekly and monthly goals. Set a fixed time where parent and child can appraise the situation.

Remember to have age-appropriate and skill-appropriate tasks. For example: If a child has problems copying their homework because of their writing pace, instead of having ten pages notes to copy at the end of each week, let them do just six at first. Check each week to encourage progress. Have a predetermined time when the child knows you're going to check so they can be ready.

Attend parent-teacher association meetings. Anytime you identify with your children's school or related experiences, your child sees that you value their education.

Don't speak disrespectfully or criticize your children's teachers in front of your child, because children can only learn from people they respect. So every time you disrespect your child's teacher—for example, talking about their clothes or scruffy shoes—unconsciously you make it difficult for your child to learn from someone they think you view as not good enough.

The top secret of school success is consistent practice

Your child's pace for learning is unique, so resist comparing them to others who are ready to leave a new concept in one day. If a topic needs review, even though the teacher is moving on to new material at school, make photocopies of the page your child had trouble with, and work through the content each evening until the concept is mastered.

Keep the home a practice-friendly space. Make adjustments as needed so each child has something that appeals to them. Choose the space that is comfortable where they have the right sitting posture to be able to sit for longer times to study.

Keep the space well-lit. Ensure fewer distractions. Most of all, show support for your child's individual learning style—whether it's visual, auditory, reading and writing, or kinesthetic. Parents can buy a tape recorder for the digital learner to record their notes. Work with visual learners to create flashcards using colored markers and sticky notes. And for auditory learners, let your child read lessons out loud.

When assisting your child with homework, remember to stop and ask questions rather than always providing answers. You can encourage conversations with the ideas from the reading, because it will help with mastery of the concepts. Above all, celebrate the little wins, because little strides create big success stories.

Last, remember to talk about sex and drugs. Do not let their peers be the only influence on your children. Ensure you have real conversations about these topics. Help your child develop the mindset of a champion.

There are two types of mindsets. A growth mindset is when somebody believes they can learn to be good and become better. They are not afraid of challenges. They continue when things get hard. They know that they have put effort in to learn, and they learn from criticism. They are also inspired by people who do well. This growth mindset helps someone who wants to learn, and makes them coachable even when they do not have any skills at the outset.

On the other hand, a fixed mindset is when someone thinks they are already good enough, they don't need to learn, and are not coachable. A fixed mindset is the opposite of growth. These people either think they're born good or born not so good. They cannot learn. They're afraid of challenges. They give up and get defensive easily. They feel criticized when given feedback, and they're threatened by people who do well.

Encourage your child to develop a growth mindset, and to always be open to learning.

REAL LIFE APPLICATION

If a child is struggling with reading in Kindergarten, most likely it will continue to be a challenge as they grow older, because they will always be a bit below grade level in reading. Consider intervening early by creating activities that encourage practice and repetition. In this case, you might allow children to read aloud to you or the family dog.

Do not make any correction whenever the child is reading. Of course, they will make mistakes like misreading words, or saying words that were not there. This is all normal.

Sometimes when we try to correct our children, they will get upset. This will occur for their friends and teachers and with other subjects and activities too. These children thought they already knew how to do everything already. They assume what the teachers are teaching should come to them easily. Well, guess what? When it's not easy, they get upset. Negative thoughts will come into their minds, such as "You suck. You can't do anything. This should be so easy." Suddenly, we see tears coming down the child's face in front of friends and teachers.

When the child can no longer control their emotions, this is where the real problem begins. You see, when children lose control of their emotions, they stop listening, and they stop thinking. The children will become difficult to those around them. And when they finally get through it, they are tired. This is not healthy, and it's not the person you want them to be. And it's also not the person they want to be.

WHAT TO DO

Our children want to know why they are feeling a certain way and why their emotions are so strong. Remind them that it's not necessary to know everything or to master every new skill the first time out. This is a perfect opportunity to talk about growth and fixed mindsets, and how to change a fixed mindset into a growth mindset.

> *Remember, it's not necessary to know everything or master every new skill the first time out!*

One way is by using the little three-letter word "yet." Whenever your child is tempted to say something like, "I can't do it," have them add the word "yet" at the end of the sentence. "I can't do it... yet." A sentence like "I don't understand" becomes "I don't understand... yet." It's the "yet" that reminds children they just need to put a little more effort in. Your child may still struggle with a fixed mindset from time to time, but each day will get a little better than the day before and the child will eventually become a champion.

Fostering strong relationships with your child is of utmost importance. The root of the word *relationship* is to relate. One thing is always constant—when parents and teens struggle to relate to one another, their relationship suffers. This increase in things like teen depression, anxiety and suicide. Suicide is the leading cause of death for children age 10–17.

Do not wait until your child is struggling. If they are isolating, not doing well in school, taking drugs, inflicting self-harm or having suicidal ideations, it means they're scared, they're desperate, and they want to know what to do. Your family can be the first line of defense, but for this to happen there's got to be a solid relationship between the parent and the teen. Therefore, I suggest you seek to create a parent-teen partnership with your child.

Avoid parenting styles that can damage the relationship between you and your child. This includes comments that sound humiliating like "What's wrong with you?" This also includes coddling like "If I buy you a new video game, will you start your assignment?" These styles have been the go-to methods for decades, but even though parents use both with good intentions to motivate and to protect their children, the message isn't being received the same way it was intended.

> *Avoid parenting styles that can damage your relationship with your child.*

The solution is the parent-teen partnership model. Unlike humiliating or pampering, partnering helps you build and strengthen your relationship with your teen. Partnering also uses a totally different language style. Instead of asking ridiculous questions, partnering statements sound like "I have the feeling you've had a rough day," or "I don't know if you'd want to talk to me about it, but if you did, I'd love to listen."

You will need to monitor, support and help your child develop good work habits without it looking like nagging. Let your child know you expect them to do well, that you believe in them and that their education matters. For example say, "I know if you work hard that you can do well. How do you think you can improve next time?" High expectations provide success more often than teaching children with flashcards or helping them with homework.

Continue to talk about school with your child. Don't just ask "How was school today?" Be specific. Let children show off their talents. They love it when they feel smarter than you. For example ask, "What was it like dissecting a frog?" "Have you thought about what courses you might want to take next year?" or "Did you get to go outside for recess today?" Talking to your child about school has a bigger impact than limiting television time or how often they go out during the week.

Next, help your child develop good work habits. A positive attitude will help shape a person's entire future. When children plan, it will also encourage them to recognize when to ask for help when they need it, and help them sail smoothly in society. Say things like "Your persistence paid off. I knew you could do it," or "We all find some things hard, but I know you can work through this," or "I can see you feel bad about the mark on that test. What do you think you could do differently next time?" Growing a positive attitude and good work habits is even more important than focusing on test scores.

Set aside time to read together. Reading is the foundation for education, so grab a book and read together often. Ask your child to sit down and cuddle while you read. Pose questions like "This book is great. What do you think will happen next?" for younger children, or with older ones consider a recommendation of "You should read this book when I'm finished. I think you'll love it."

Children whose parents read to them at an early age are more likely to love reading and do better in both mathematics and spelling by the time they're 16 years old. Remember the act of reading is more important than focusing on phonics.

School and homework can be a challenge for children and for parents. You are not a homework policeman or a substitute teacher. Instead tell children you expect that they will work hard and do their best. Talk with them about school, help them develop good work habits to persist even when the going gets tough and encourage them to love reading. Talk with your children and leave the nagging and micromanaging behind. You are more likely to have a successful student with a great atmosphere at home.

If you need to advocate for your children, do not feel like your parenting skills are on trial. It's important that you understand your role. Parents are the very first educators. They have the most vested in their children to make sure they get the best education. As a parent, you know your children, and you do not need to feel intimidated or judged. Come in informed and ready to talk about the situation. For example, if your child receives low grades yet they spend five hours doing homework every night, the school need to know that, so that they can make a better and more appropriate plan for your child.

In Summary

Throughout this book you have learned ways to assist your child on the way to academic success. These include parental involvement at home, monitoring schoolwork, establishing open communication with your child and your child's school, and finally through positive parental involvement at school, always with the goal of supporting and encouraging your child to strive for more.

We all want to see our children succeed, both academically and in life. As well as reminding your child that it's not necessary to be perfect or to get everything right the first time, remind yourself that parenting is a process. We all make mistakes along the way. Focus on creating loving relationships that support your child, and you will be more than halfway there!

Optimize Your 15 Minutes a Day
so that you and your child can
Win the Day... Everyday!

Visit 15MinutesADayBook.com/Win

REFERENCES

Altschul, I. (2011). Parental involvement and the academic achievement of Mexican American youths: What kinds of involvement in youths' education matter most? *Social Work Research, 35*(3), 159–170.

Brizius, J. A., & Foster, S. A. (1993). *Generation to generation: Realizing the promise of family literacy.* High Scope Press.

Dearing, E., H. Kreider, S. Simpkins, & Weiss. H. (2006). Family involvement in school and low-income children's literacy: Longitudinal associations between and within families. *Journal of Educational Psychology, 98*(4): 653–664.

Dornbusch, S., Ritter, P., Leiderman, P., Roberts, D., & Fraleigh, M. (1987). The relation of parenting style to adolescent school performance. *Child Development, 58*(5), 1244–1257.

Epstein, J. L., & Sanders, M. G. (2000). Connecting home, school, and community. New directions for social research. In M. T. Hallinan (Ed.), *Handbook of the Sociology of Education* (pp. 285–306). New York, NY: Kluwer Academic/Plenum Publishers.

Fan, X., & Chen, M. (2001). Parental involvement and students' academic achievement: A meta-analysis. *Educational Psychology Review, 13*(1), 1–22.

Georgiou, S. N., & Tourva, A. (2007). Parental attributions and parental involvement. *Social Psychology Education, 10*, 473–482.

Herrold, K., & O'Donnell, K. (2008). Parent and family involvement in education, 2006–07 School Year, From the National Household Education Surveys Program of 2007 (NCES 2008-050). Washington, DC: National Center for Education Statistics, Institute of Education Sciences, U.S. Department of Education.

Hoover-Dempsey, K.V., & Sandler, H.M. (1995). Parental involvement in children's education: Why does it make a difference? *Teachers College Record, 95*, 310–331.

Jasso, J. (2007). *African American and non-Hispanic White parental involvement in the education of elementary school-aged children.* Syracuse, NY: Syracuse University.

Jeynes, W. (2007). The relationship between parental involvement and urban secondary school student academic achievement: A meta-analysis. *Urban Education, 42* (1),82–109.

Jones, N., & Schneider, B. (2009). Rethinking the role of parenting: Promoting adolescent academic success and emotional well-being. In N. E. Hill & R. K. Chao (Eds.), *Families, schools, and the adolescent: Connecting research, policy, and practice* (pp. 73–90). New York, NY: Teachers College Press.

Lee, J., & Bowen, N. K. (2006). Parent involvement, cultural capital, and the achievement gap among elementary school children. *American Educational Research Journal, 43*, 193–218.

Magnuson, K., & Waldfogel, J. (2008). *Steady gains and stalled progress: Inequality and the Black-White test score gap.* New York, NY: Russell Sage Foundation.

Reay, D. (1998). Cultural reproduction: Mothers involvement in their children's primary schooling. In M. Grenfell & D. James (Eds.), *Bourdieu and education: Acts of practical theory* (pp. 55–71). Bristol, PA: Falmer.

Ramey, C.T., Ramey, S.L. (2004). Early learning and school readiness: Can early intervention make a difference? *Merrill-Palmer Quarterly, 50*(4), 471–491.

Sheldon, S.B., & Epstein, J.L. (2007). *Parent and student surveys of family and community involvement in the elementary and middle grades.* Baltimore, MD: Center on School, Family, and Community

Trotman, M. F. (2001). Involving African American parents: Recommendations to increase the level of parent involvement with African American families. *The Journal of Negro Education, 70,* 275–285.

Weiss, H. B., Mayer, E., Kreider, H., Vaughan, M., Dearing, E., Hencke, R., & Pinto, K. (2003). Making it work: Low-income working mothers' involvement in their children's education. *American Educational Research Journal,* 40(4), 879–901.

Willis, M. G. (1998). We are family: Creating success in an African American public elementary school. Unpublished Doctoral Dissertation: Georgia State University, Atlanta.

GET YOUR 15 MINUTES A DAY
FREE BONUS CHECKLIST
Get on Track for As, Bs, & Honor Roll...

QUICK AND EASY

- Put Your Bedtime Routine on Autopilot, so that you rest easy at the end of the day
- Develop Responsibility in Your Child, so that he or she can drive his or her own progress
- Connect with Your Child Each Day, so that you can understand what's really important to them
- Organize Your Morning Routine, so that your child is ready to Win the Day
- Instill a Positive Work Ethic in Your Child, so that they are ready to suceed at home & at school
- Reward Yourself & Your Child, so that you are both motivated to make these new habits permanent

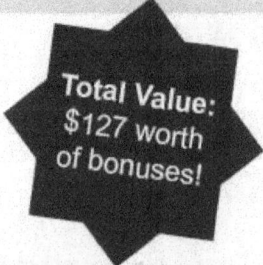

Total Value: $127 worth of bonuses!

15MinutesADayBook.com/Win

About the Author

DR. FRANCISCA ENIH was born in Ibadan, Oyo State, Nigeria, the first of eleven children. Growing up, she was fascinated with taking care of the needy, and this interest led to early exposure to Saint Vincent De Paul Society, since she was drawn to stories related to caring. During the devasting Hurricane Katrina in August 2005, she served as President of the Nigerian Catholic Ministry at Saint Albert of Trapani Catholic Church in Houston, Texas. One of the missions was to help the needy, providing hot meals to individuals displaced by the hurricane. Later, Dr. Enih, who now teaches Skills for Living and Learning at the middle school level, developed a passion for ideas. She took professional developments in science, technology, mathematics and engineering and in 2007-2008 school year was named Houston Geological Society Earth Science Teacher of the Year from Rice University, Houston, Texas, and Houston Independent School District Cream of the Crop in 2007. In 2008 and 2009 she was elected Holland Middle School Special Education Teacher of the Year. Also, she is certified to teach English as a Second Language.

Dr. Enih, who lives in Houston, Texas, has been an educator since 1997. She earned her Doctorate from Texas Southern University and her dissertation title is "The Relationship Between Parental Involvement and Middle School Student Achievement in Mathematics." She is currently the Parish Pastoral Council member of St. Albert Catholic Church. Her goal is to uphold human self-esteem, to always be patient, and to promote fairness and kindness.

www.ingramcontent.com/pod-product-compliance
Lightning Source LLC
LaVergne TN
LVHW041547070426
835507LV00011B/966